# HIS LOVE

## *Compels*

# HIS LOVE
## Compels

The Sacrificial Message of
God from the New Testament

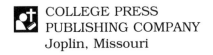

Thomas H. Olbricht

COLLEGE PRESS
PUBLISHING COMPANY
Joplin, Missouri

# $\mathcal{T}$able of Contents

To my Pepperdine University students,

1986–

both in Malibu and off campus.

Among these I single out Ronald R. Cox,

who read the manuscript in its entirety,

and helped eliminate certain errors and infelicities.

# 1
# Why They Wrote

*T*he story line of the New Testament is an astounding declaration of love. It speaks of God's love and our love. The account compels because God's love is unexpected, unrelenting, and unfathomable. In reading of God's actions in Christ through the eyes and hearts of those with whom he walked and ate, we are overwhelmed by the depictions and conclusions drawn. When it finally dawns on us what Jesus did on our behalf, we are astonished and affirmed. Our life is never the same again. We are compelled to love because of his love.

Paul, who was confronted by the risen Lord on the Damascus road, wrote a clear and incisive statement as to why it is that Christ's love compels us.

> **For Christ's love compels us, because we are convinced that one died for all, and therefore all died. And he died for all, that those who live should no longer live for themselves but for him who died for them and was raised again (2 Cor. 5:14-15, NIV).**

God began this unprecedented action by sending his only Son, conceived by the Holy Spirit in the womb of Mary,

7

a woman. This same Son, God consigned to death on the cross, but in an astonishing show of power raised him up. God did it, not just to prove his might, but as a display of compassion for sin-inflicted humankind. Christ's resurrection assures ours. "We know that the one who raised the Lord Jesus will raise us also with Jesus . . . ." (2 Cor. 4:14). This same Son, God will send to end history, and bring all those who are his into his very presence.

## *The New Testament as a Sequel*

The New Testament is a sequel to an earlier report on the mighty acts of God — the Old Testament. But it is more than a sequel. The story of Jesus of Nazareth and the apostolic witness to his resurrection bring to fruition God's ultimate act, thereby demonstrating once for all his inexplicable love. In *He Loves Forever* the author traced the steadfast, unfailing love of God through two thousand years of human history. In the Old Testament we discovered many occasions in which God exhibited empathy for humankind entangled in the web of worldly existence. We were forced to consider at length, then marvel at the fact that God never gives up on man made in his image, but God's promise of continuation seemed unrealized.

We finished the Old Testament, but we were still not fully cognizant of how all this will be resolved. The plaintive cry of the prophet remained in our ears.

> For thus says the LORD:
> Your hurt is incurable,
>     your wound is grievous.
> There is no one to uphold your cause,
>     no medicine for your wound,
>     no healing for you.
> Why do you cry out over your hurt?
>     Your pain is incurable.

> Because your guilt is great,
>> because your sins are so numerous,
>> I have done these things to you (Jer. 30:12-13,15).

We are undone at the charges. We know they are true. At the same time, we live in hope. The Old Testament hints in many places that there is a way out. We cry out to know what it is. There must be a remedy! But what is it? We take up the New Testament in anticipation that a major announcement will be made in regard to an astounding cure. And we are not disappointed.

## *Finishing the Unfinished*

In sending the Son, God more than reveals a loving disposition. He is more than a deity who loves to reach out and touch someone. He makes it clear, despite certain characterizations of the biblical God to the contrary, that he is not the sort to hold his universe and man in it at arm's length. He constantly reaches out and embraces all that is his. But more importantly, in sending the Son, he provides a remedy for the age-old scourge of human rebelliousness. The good news is that Jesus Christ, through his death and resurrection, is the cure for human perversity. The prophets anguished over that ailment but concluded that man neither possesses the remedy nor can he through frenzied research develop one. The only hope lies with God. As master of the universe and maker of all that is, including man, he has the prerogative to redo man. What man cannot do, God accomplishes. That, according to the prophets, is the only road out.

Paul has a way of putting it which reminds one of just how good the news is.

> For while we were still weak, at the right time Christ died for the ungodly. Indeed, rarely will anyone die for a righteous person — though perhaps for a good person someone might actually dare to die. But God proves his love for us in that while we still were sinners Christ died for us (Rom. 5:6-8).

For Paul the bedrock of the gospel is that "Christ died for our sins in accordance with the scriptures, and that he was buried, and that he was raised on the third day" (1 Cor. 15:3). Paul felt himself at one with the prophets in declaring man corrupted to the extent that prospects for reconciliation are nonexistent apart from decisive action on God's part. So he cried out. "Wretched man that I am! Who will rescue me from this body of death?" (Rom. 7:24). Unlike the prophets, however, Paul affirmed the concrete way in which God himself came to the rescue. The way out is achieved. "Thanks be to God through Jesus Christ our Lord!" (Rom. 7:25). Jesus is the solution to sin. He is the fantastic remedy the prophets anticipated!

What is enigmatic in the Old, the New Testament sets forth in bold relief. God demonstrated his love in a concrete, for all to see, action in the ministry, death, and resurrection of Jesus Christ. Old Testament *chesed* (Hebrew for "God's steadfast love") pointed over the horizon and beyond itself. In an astonishing development, *chesed* was concretized and fully realized in the person of Jesus. He emerged as the focal point of God's love. When he appeared, and upon exhibiting his amazing power, people said, "God has come to help his people" (Luke 7:16, NIV). All earlier displays of God's loving action paled by comparison. "No one has ever seen God. It is God the only Son, who is close to the Father's heart, who has made him known," declared John, who saw him, touched him, and heard him (John 1:18; 1 John 1:1-3).

Beyond the shadow of a doubt, Jesus is the focus — the story line of the New Testament. The message of the New Testament is not about an idea. It is about a person — Jesus the truth of God. "I am the way, and the truth, and the life. No one comes to the Father except through me." (John 14:6) When we see him as he is, we have cut to the heart of the New Testament, as he also cuts to our heart (Acts 2:37; Heb. 4:12-13).

## *The Task Ahead*

The structuring and fleshing out of the message, or theology, of the New Testament is a detailed and meticulous task. Ostensibly, Jesus stands irreplaceably at the center of that message even though some scholars have argued for other centers. Who do the New Testament writers conceive him to be? What do the authors of these works think he accomplished? What are the ramifications of these amazing historical developments for the life of humankind? Reaching out for the answers in a somewhat systematic way is the goal of *His Love Compels*.

The reasons for which the books of the New Testament came to be written supply us with an insight into the core of its message. These reasons revolve about the conviction that Jesus is a new and unprecedented inbreaking of God into human history. After tracking the formation of the New Testament we can go on to set out a method for detailing the claims concerning Jesus in a somewhat organized manner so that they flesh out his central role in early Christianity.

## *The New Action of God*

The air was filled with excitement and anticipation. From various quarters men and women hoped beyond hope — cried out desperately for a decisive inbreaking of God. Life was bleak and governments oppressive. Relief was insufficient from any human resource. The only possible avenue for a turnaround, so it seemed, lay with a new work of the God who had acted so mightily for his people in the past.

In the minds of Palestinian Jews, the reign of Herod the Great represented the fruition of past blunders, inequities, and defeat. The whole Mediterranean was controlled from a distance by Rome's emperor and celebrated Senate. These officials had their own agendas. They cared little for the aspirations and problems peculiar to Palestine. They did not respect nor desire to understand the Jewish faith. Governors were social and political climbers. Many local officials were corrupt and immoral. The governors cared little about the intrigues and oppressions in Palestine as long as the officials kept order and handed over the tax revenues. The taxes were high and often unjust.

Attitudes about the oppressors varied, but for those who addressed God as sovereign of the universe, relief was expected from only one source — God himself. In the past when Israel was down and out, she cried to Yahweh in desperation (Exod. 2:23; Judg. 3:15) As a result, Yahweh (The Hebrew name for God in the Old Testament, translated "LORD") heard and came to the rescue. When his people humbled themselves, when they recognized their own inability to overcome, when they cried their heart out to him, Yahweh moved swiftly and decisively. His mercy and forgiveness was profound as well as continual. God's *chesed* did not depend on the heart nor the action of man. Had it, nothing would have resulted. It depended rather on God's constant yearning for fellowship with man made in his image. The time was ripe for God to change the headlines. The dawn of a new day eagerly waited just over the horizon.

The God of Israel does not disappoint. The Father of the Lord Jesus Christ never leaves in the lurch those who are his. He never turns his back on those who wait (Isa. 30:18). God exhibited his love to the descendants of Abraham in a surprising and completely unexpected manner. At first even they did not comprehend. Then they were alternately shocked and speechless. But after years of seeing, hearing, and reflecting, they came to an amazing conclusion. Certain ones among them became convinced that God himself in an inexplicable manner lived in their very midst in Jesus, born of Mary in Bethlehem, and later attaining adulthood in Nazareth. By participating in what happened at the Sea of Galilee, on well-worn pathways, and in Jerusalem, they arrived at the conviction that in Jesus, Son of God, Yahweh displayed his ultimate love. "For God so loved the world that he gave his only Son" (John 3:16). He is a God who can be counted on when the going gets rough. He always has at heart the best interests of humankind. He always comes through in astounding and unexpected ways.

## A Story to Tell

What were these people to do who walked with, ate with, and listened to Jesus? They arrived at the surprising conclusion that Jesus was, is, and always will be Son of God, the anointed one, the promised king for God's people. Believing as they did, they could not keep quiet. Peter, an outspoken leader among them, when told by the officials to keep his views to himself, responded, "Whether it is right in God's sight to listen to you rather than to God, you must judge; for we cannot keep from speaking about what we have seen and heard" (Acts 4:19,20).

So they told neighbors, relatives, and friends about their astonishing experiences with this man sent from God. They told of his compassion. They recounted the times his heart reached out to widows, lepers, and the blind. They reported that he called God "Father," and invited others to call him "our Father." They repeated his parables about the kingdom of God, its proximity, its obstacles, yet its unprecedented growth. These oral accounts echoed in the hamlets of Galilee, in the streets and houses of Jerusalem, then in the villages round about.

The believers stayed in Jerusalem for a time, encouraging each other, working out ramifications, and discipling the new converts. But news of Jesus' astounding resurrection spread abroad. It could not be contained. Within a few years Christians traveled the major thoroughfares of the empire, relating the surprising turn of events as they went (Acts 2:8-11).

They walked north into Samaria. They rode donkeys to Caesarea, and booked passage on grain boats headed for Antioch, a major east-west trade center. A few years later believers could be found sharing the good news in Asia Minor, Greece, Egypt, and even the imperial capitol — Rome. They invited men and women at all strata to accept Jesus as the resurrected Son of God. Should they believe in the Nazarene as sent from heaven, God in return would adopt them as sons and daughters. He would welcome them into his kingly sway, and shower on them his good gifts.

In major cities, and along the trade routes, multitudes of women and men joyfully received the fantastic news. These believers in each locale became a conclave of Christians — a support group for persons of like faith. They met regularly and especially on the landmark day when God raised Jesus from the tomb — Sunday, the first day of the week. Soon through much of the eastern empire, small house assemblies ("gatherings of the Lord," *kyriakos*, brought into English as "church") dotted the towns and countryside. These disciples gladly heard the stories of what Jesus said and did.

As the years went by, certain of the eye witnesses, designated by Jesus as "apostles," that is, from the Greek, "those sent," put their accounts on papyrus or vellum. Those who responded requested a more permanent record. Likewise, other believers, perhaps to share the glad tidings with distant relatives, or to put into writing the accounts of eye witnesses, wrote additional reports. Luke wrote of these various accounts (Luke 1:1-4). There was much to tell. The story needed adaptation to persons of all sorts. These writers set out to accommodate the insatiable desire to know as much as possible about Jesus.

We do not know exactly who wrote first, or which part of the gospel made it to papyrus ahead of the rest. It seems likely, however, that the earliest written accounts were apostolic, and focused on the details of those final crucial days leading to the death and resurrection of the Lord. Then later, in response to the demand, others both early and later added details about Jesus' mighty works, his parables, his sermons, and his sayings. The appellation "Gospel" (*euangelion*) became widespread for these accounts. As the years wore on, these accounts were elaborated, polished, and put into the form in which they have come down to us in the four Gospels. God through his Holy Spirit breathed upon these writings. They indeed became his very Word concerning the accomplishments of his Son on human behalf — his inscripturated report to a lost and dying world. Along with, and perhaps as early as, the initial versions of the gospel, were the apostolic efforts to set out specific ramifications of God's visit in the Son. These resulted in epistles, discourses, and an apocalypse. They were directed to either church leaders or to the churches themselves as they attempted to put into practice the style of life recommended by Jesus.

These privileged manuscripts, that is Gospels, epistles, and discourses, circulated separately at first. After a few decades they were collected, preserved, and designated, "The New Testament." These documents were assigned this impressive appellation because those who collected them believed that the God of the exodus in a new and vital way entered history in Jesus and demonstrated concretely and once for all his intense and steadfast love for humankind.

The Christians revered this new collection and elevated it to the same status as the Hebrew Scriptures. Already before the collection was complete Paul's letters were so designated.

> So also our beloved brother Paul wrote to you according to the wisdom given him, speaking of this as he does in all his letters. There are some things in them hard to understand, which the ignorant and unstable twist to their own destruction, as they do the other scriptures (2 Pet. 3:15-16).

❧

But in comparison with the Hebrew Scriptures these had a new focus, or better still, a new person — Jesus Son of God and only Savior. These documents centered on who he was, what he did, what he said, and the implications of all this for obedience and discipleship. The Old Testament spoke of God, his desire for human companionship, his promises and laws. But the "new" Scriptures reported a new, intimate relationship with God made possible through trust in the Son. In them is found the compelling story of God's appearance in human flesh in Jesus of Nazareth, Son of Man and Son of God. The message of the New Testament is, for that reason, inextricably woven out of, and around God's person in Jesus. The New Testament in its theology has nothing to do with abstract, philosophical theology. It is a person-centered theology, that is, the theology of the personhood of God, and ramifications of that personhood for our own.

## *The Heart of the New Testament*

In setting forth the manner in which the New Testament came about we have identified the heart of its message. In academic circles the enterprise upon which we are embarked is called "New Testament Theology."

In the twentieth century New Testament theologians have located the center of the New Testament variously. For some it is the church (ecclesiology).[1] For others it is the mighty salvific acts of God (*heilsgeschichte*).[2] For others still, it is this or that view pertaining to Jesus (Christology).[3] A

---

[1] Alan Richardson, *An Introduction to the Theology of the New Testament* (New York: Harper, 1959).

[2] Ethelbert Stauffer, *New Testament Theology* (London: SCM, 1963). Oscar Cullmann, *Christ and Time*, 3rd edition (London: SCM, 1967); *Salvation in History* (New York: Harper, 1967). George Eldon Ladd, *A Theology of the New Testament* (Grand Rapids: Eerdmans, 1974, 1993).

[3] Vincent Taylor, *The Formation of the Gospel Tradition* (London: Macmillan,

fourth group following the German school of Rudolf Bultmann, locate man as the center (anthropology).[4] Donald Guthrie has decided, since in his view a center is not immediately apparent, that the best approach is to take up the traditional topics of systematic theology such as faith, the Scriptures, God, the Holy Spirit, the church, salvation, and eschatology.[5]

It is my conviction, some of these experts to the contrary, that Jesus is the focal point for all the reflection and comment in the New Testament writings. These documents were first written and then collected because of the unique way in which God's inexplicable love is demonstrated through Jesus' deeds and words. The focus of the New Testament is not a body of doctrine, a set of laws and rules, or a series of propositions. The focus is a man, Jesus the Galilean. In these writings one finds the implications of his life for our life. The key to the message of the New Testament is that the ultimate and concrete *chesed* of God comes to fruition in Jesus, Son and Savior. With him present the kingdom of God is among us (Luke 17:21).

## The Spotlight Is on Jesus!

It is not enough, however, to locate Jesus as the fulcrum of the message. Down through the centuries the views about him have been legion, as Albert Schweitzer documented in

---

1957); *The Atonement in New Testament Teaching* (London: Epworth, 1958). Eduard Schweizer, *Jesus* (Richmond, VA: John Knox, 1971). Peter Balla, *Challenges to New Testament Theology* (Peabody, MA: Hendrickson, 1998).

[4] Rudolf Bultmann, *Theology of the New Testament*, 2 vols. (New York: Scribners, 1951, 1955) Hans Conzelmann, *An Outline of the Theology of the New Testament* (New York: Harper, 1969).

[5] Donald Guthrie, *New Testament Theology* (Downers Grove: InterVarsity, 1981).

*The Quest for the Historical Jesus* (1910). We are interested in who the writers of the New Testament considered Jesus to be. We wish to seek out their perspective on his actions, his accomplishments and his place in the sun. We are not concerned with the christology of Martin Luther, John Calvin, Friedrich Schleiermacher, or Paul Tillich. We are searching for the christology of Mark, John, Peter and Paul. We aspire to know what they believed about Jesus and why they wrote and acted as they did.

Sometimes New Testament theologians write as if they have a license to create Jesus out of their own presuppositions and fertile imagination. It is as if they have been handed a dotted outline of Jesus' image and told to color him in as they wish. I do not construe such liberty permissible. I object to a work flying the flag of New Testament theology and then submitting the christology of its author. If it is New Testament christology, it should set out the theology of Paul, Luke, and John. Albert Schweitzer concluded that many biographies on Jesus in the latter half of the nineteenth century revealed more about the author than about Jesus. These works are like a person looking in a well and seeing their own reflection. It is my intention in this work to set forth the Jesus of the New Testament as best I am able, and eschew unique personal insights that originate from elsewhere than the New Testament.

## *Major Topics in a New Testament Theology*

Jesus obviously shines through page after page of the New Testament. The topics of New Testament theology are therefore the significant features of what he did and said. What are these topics? Shall they be selected according to current theological interests, whether the Holy Spirit, marriage and family, or women's roles?

It is interesting to scrutinize portraits of Jesus in various epochs. The paintings typically reflect the manner of dress and the artistic modes of their time. The same may be said of theologians whose word-pictures ring true to the century in which they are written. Jesus has been depicted as an authoritarian, a purveyor of superior ethical norms, one with a true conception of deity, a loving shepherd, a miracle worker, a divine man, a sage, an apocalyptic prophet, a perceiver of existential reality, and as a deity who only appeared to be human.

We are interested in a New Testament theology, not a twentieth century theology. We must therefore follow the lead of those who first knew Jesus — those who walked and ate with him. These early disciples not only outlined his life, they put into bold relief the items of greatest importance. We must not fall into the trap, however compelling, of supposing that every incident in the life of Jesus is of equal weight, for example, that the feeding of the five thousand is right up there on a parity with the resurrection.

## A Flat View of Scripture

A popular conception of Scripture may be labeled a "flat view" since with this way of thinking every item is said to be of equal weight and consequence. This position is presupposed by the person who says, for example, that John 14:1-3 is his favorite passage, then hastens to add that one should not have a favorite Scripture since all are of equal significance. A person with this frame of mind is fearful that the deceitful or naive will pick and choose among matters to be obeyed or believed. A case in point is Thomas Jefferson. Jefferson, as the result of his deistic predilections, was embarrassed by the miracle stories. He accordingly published for friends a New Testament with all the miracles deleted. The fear is real that if each of us is left to decide what is most important, we will come down strongly on those features at which we excel and which meet our interests.

The concerns of those who hold a flat view of Scripture are justified. Their arguments seem logical and forceful. Unfortunately for them, however, their position is supported by neither Jesus nor Paul. Jesus issued a clarion call for identifying matters of utmost importance.

> "Woe to you, scribes and Pharisees, hypocrites! For you tithe mint, dill, and cummin, and have neglected the weightier matters of the law: justice and mercy and faith. It is these you ought to have practiced without neglecting the others" (Matt. 23:23).

Paul identified actions of Jesus which are at the forefront and more important than others.

> For I handed on to you as of first importance what I in turn received: that Christ died for our sins in accordance with the scriptures, and that he was buried, and that he was raised on the third day in accordance with the scriptures, and that he appeared to Cephas, then to the twelve (1 Cor. 15:3-5).

Neither Jesus nor Paul held the flat view of scripture.

How then do we visualize Scripture so that each individual does not arbitrarily assign significance according to personal prejudice. An analogy from money may be of help. Money comes in various amounts running from pennies to ten thousand dollar bills. No one would dream of assigning the same value to each and every piece of money. At the same time no one would argue that dimes lose their value in a system where one hundred bills are worth more. Even in a system of hierarchical values, the lowest entity on the spectrum has worth. I grew up during the great depression. In 1935 I could buy a Baby Ruth, as much as I could eat at once, all for a penny. A penny buys much less today, but still is worth something. If I see a penny in a parking lot or on a sidewalk I have to be in a terrible hurry not to bend over and pick it up.

Now it strikes me that what we really want to hold out for biblically is not that everything in Scripture is of equal weight, but that everything is of value. Nothing is to be discarded.

Neither you, I, nor anyone else has the prerogative of concluding that a detail in Scripture is worthless. Jesus himself made
that point. "It is these you ought to have practiced without
neglecting the others." Setting aside a tenth of the garden dill
has merit, but not nearly as much as showing mercy.

The question remains, however, as to how more importance is to be assigned. Is establishing a hierarchy purely arbi-
trary? No! The matter obviously cannot be left up to each
individual to work out as he or she pleases. The whole question is to be decided by regard for apostolic declaration. We
will make headway by raising once again the question as to
what are the topics about Jesus. The answer is not to come
from within ourselves, but from the apostolic witness.

The important topics pertaining to Jesus may be discovered in the basic declarations as to the centers of the faith,
the apostolic sermons, and the hymnic materials, such as
1 Timothy 3:16. The most complete outlines are located in
the Acts sermons [2:17-36; 4:8-12; 7:1-35; 10:34-43; 13:16-
41, and 17:16-31]. The most complete is Peter's sermon to
Cornelius and his household. Several years ago C.H. Dodd
pointed out that the outline of Peter's sermon may be super-
imposed upon the Gospel of Mark.[6] The gospel story is therefore fleshed out from the basic apostolic preaching.

By drawing upon Peter's sermon we identify the following topics from within the New Testament. (1) Jesus the Son
of God came in the flesh, (2) he was heralded by John the
Baptist, (3) he was anointed by the Holy Spirit, (4) he went
about doing good, (5) he preached good news, (6) he gave his
life as a ransom for many, (7) he was raised for our justification, (8) witnesses set out to announce his amazing resurrection, (9) his ministry continued under the auspices of the

[6] C.H. Dodd, *The Apostolic Preaching and Its Developments* (London: Hodder
and Stoughton, 1936).

Holy Spirit, (10) he called the church into being, (11) he showed no partiality, and (12) he is coming back to claim his own. These topics are not ours; they are apostolic. We have therefore deferred to the apostles to pinpointing of those matters which are of highest importance to the Christian faith.

The topics about Jesus are those so identified by the earliest believers who sat spellbound as they heard his words, walked with him on dusty pathways, and shared bread, fish, and cheese. They are the ones so declared by New Testament authors, and the earliest witnesses to Jesus' life and teachings.

## *His Love Compels Us*

We conclude these remarks on the heart of the New Testament and how it is to be fleshed out with the question, "What is the overall significance of these topics for you and me?" The answer is that because of the profound love God exhibited in the death and resurrection of Jesus we arrive face to face with the amazing fact that God is not some detached, impersonal, granite-faced power in the universe. Rather he is a God who works incessantly, day and night, to reach out and touch humankind. He entered the very arena where humans struggle, work, love, and hurt. He came. He lived humbly as a man. He set in motion the arrangements whereby men and women are welcome to fall in pace with God for an intimate walk. Because God gave his only Son, I know on whom I can count. I can count on God to work creatively and lovingly for my welfare, security, and position. I can count on God to always be there. As long as I go with God, he will go with me. He went with me even before I accepted his invitation. He continues to lovingly push me along even when I am inclined to turn aside. He never gives up. "No, in all these things we are more than conquerors through him who loved us" (Rom. 8:37). Because God so openly and unreservedly loved us while we were yet sinners, we are compelled by his love. We are captivated and captured by Him. We are empowered to his kind of life in response to his unrelenting love.

# Questions for Discussion

1. Why does the Old Testament seem unfinished?

2. What is the central story line of the New Testament?

3. Why did the New Testament authors write the documents they produced?

4. Did stories about Jesus circulate before the New Testament Gospels were written? How and why?

5. Who do you think wrote the first of the four Gospels?

6. What is the heart of the New Testament?

7. Is it appropriate for people to color in their own picture of Jesus?

8. Is a flat view of Scripture biblical?

9. What did Paul declare was of most importance?

10. What did Jesus set out as weightier?

11. Does every Scripture have some importance?

12. Can our life before God be understood as being compelled by the love of Christ?

# 2
# Jesus Came in the Flesh

*The* significance of Jesus is who he is, not just what he said and did. He keeps surfacing in the New Testament because of the universal claim of its authors that in some unique sense he came from God. Through its long history, Israel welcomed several highly talented, God-fearing leaders. The lawgiver, Moses; the psalm writer, David; the empire builder, Solomon; and the introspective lamenter, Jeremiah, come to mind. The Greeks and Romans acknowledged several heroes: Demosthenes, the silver-tongued orator; Alexander, the world conqueror; Cicero, the peerless statesman; and Julius Caesar, the flamboyant military genius. None of these men of distinction, however, came directly from God. Jesus was one of a kind.

## *God Alone*

Through the centuries various representations of Jesus' claim to divinity have made their way into print. Even Jesus' contemporaries understood him variously. Jesus could have been a person with a high self image and the audacity to go out on a limb. The scribes from among the Pharisees saw him exactly in that light. They charged that he took over the prerogatives of God (Mark 2:7). He presumed more than is appropriate for any human.

Jesus' relatives and friends seemed particularly disturbed that he didn't spend more time straightening out the crowds. They were especially alienated by group enthusiasm and persistence. The crowds didn't always have an opinion as to who he was, but they were excited by what he did. They saw lame persons walking, withered limbs restored, the blind receiving sight, demoniacs restored to their right minds, and the dead raised. Several from among them sensed the Spirit of God at work. The synoptic Gospels ["the look alikes": Matthew, Mark, and Luke] unanimously report that Jesus' actions and teaching disturbed his friends and relatives. He was no longer the fine young man they had known, who, though interested in the affairs of God, spent his days working with wood.

These people who knew Jesus so well wanted him to be adamant in denying divine roots. They could handle it if he came off as an extraordinary person who toyed with profound ideas and who held out a compassionate hand to all comers. They would have rejoiced at the good fortune of being identified with such a man. What upset them were the implications and opinions going beyond that. Jesus, upon setting aside twelve of his followers for a special ministry, returned home. People flocked in from all directions. They came out of the woodwork. They were so demanding that Jesus didn't even have time to eat.

That was just too much for Jesus' long-standing acquaintances. "When his family heard it, they went out to restrain him, for people were saying, 'He has gone out of his mind'" (Mark 3:21). But Jesus turned them aside, and upset them even more. After excitement over his wonders fanned into flames in the cities of Galilee, Jesus returned home once again. Now wherever Jesus went, the crowds showed up. His mother and brothers arrived to dissuade him. "And looking at those who sat around him, he said, 'Here are my mother and my brothers! Whoever does the will of God is my brother and sister and mother'" (Mark 3:34,35). Had Jesus become a military hero or a rabbi of renown, the hometown would have rolled out the red carpet. Quite apparently more was at stake. One must presume claims of divine origins on someone's part to make any sense out of all the disturbance. Jesus grew up right there before their very eyes. He was a good ole' hometown boy. But now the people who knew Jesus best grew more and more disturbed, and some downright antagonistic.

> They said, "Where did this man get all this? What is this wisdom that has been given to him? What deeds of power are being done by his hands! Is not this the carpenter, the son of Mary and brother of James and Joses and Judas and Simon, and are not his sisters here with us?" And they took offense at him (Mark 6:2-3).

But what if Jesus was in fact unique? What if his origins began with God? Mark's reasons for pointing out the negative reactions of Jesus' contemporaries was to highlight the fact that the time came when, after initiating the Galilean ministry, those who knew Jesus best were disturbed by a change. His friends and relatives sized up his words and actions as absurd, precisely because they presumed his origins were the same as those of everyone else they knew. Mark wants to challenge these misconceptions. Jesus is not like everyone else. He came from God. He is the Son of God (Mark 1:1).

It is one thing if Jesus was bold, calm, confident, compassionate, taught high moral principles, and was concerned for people of all sorts, rich and poor alike. His impact on history is justified on that ground alone. But if Jesus came from God, we are in an altogether different ball game. If Jesus came from God, he had privileged, inside information unavailable elsewhere. If Jesus came from God, he had unlimited powers and resources at his command. If Jesus came from God, the manner in which he related to people and what he said and did, disclosed more about God himself than we can ever hope to know from any other source. No wonder John, who declared that God sent Jesus, exclaimed "No one has ever seen God. It is God the only Son, who is close to the Father's heart, who has made him known" (John 1:18).

Clearly Jesus was seen as someone special from God by the Gospel writers. But he was not a deity who merely assumed a human body whenever he made periodic visits to earth as the residents of Lystra presumed in the case of Zeus and Hermes. "The gods have come down to us in human form" (Acts 14:11). Rather, he was born of woman (Gal. 4:4). Or as declared in the Gospel of John, "And the Word became flesh and lived among us, and we have seen his glory, the glory as of a father's only son" (John 1:14). He slept (Mark 4:38), as did others, and sought solitude (Mark 1:35). He was often invited to meals and ate along with the others, being hungry. (Mark 2:15; 11:12; 14:18). He walked with his followers (Mark 11:27), rode on boats (Mark 5:21) and at least in one case rode on a donkey (Mark 11:7). As his death approached, he was beaten (Mark14:65) and flogged (Mark 15:15) and thirsted (Mark 15:36); he cried out before he breathed his last (Mark 15:37); and his body was placed in a tomb (Mark 15:46). Truly he was Son of God in the flesh.

## *Son of Man*

The formulation of Chalcedon (A.D. 451) declared that Jesus is "perfect both in deity and also in humanness; this selfsame one is also actually God and actually man with a rational soul and a body."[1] The Gospels did indeed declare Jesus' humanness along with his divinity. Some have believed

---

[1] "The Definition of Chalcedon" in *Creeds of the Churches*, ed. John H. Leith (Atlanta: John Knox, 1977), pp. 35-36.

that Jesus, in his favorite self designation "Son of Man," asserted his humanness. In the Old Testament the term normally was a substitute for humankind or a man. Psalm 8:4 declared, "What is man that thou art mindful of him, and the son of man that thou dost care for him" (RSV). Since man and son of man are parallel, it is obvious that the referent is identical, that is son of man is man. Also in Ezekiel "son of man" as a manner of addressing the prophet affirms his humanness (Ezek. 2:1,3,6,8; 3:1,3,4,10,17). Even in Mark 3:28 "sons of men" is a manner of designating humans.

Jesus likely employed "Son of Man" so as to identify himself with humans, but in several contexts his divine prerogatives are more obvious than his humanness. The first time Jesus employed Son of man in the Gospel of Mark was when he announced to the paralytic let down from the roof that his sins were forgiven (Mark 2:5,10). That, according to the scribes, was a privilege belonging to God alone. When he declared the Son of Man to be Lord of the sabbath (Mark 3:8), he likewise preempted for himself the action of God, who consecrated the sabbath (Gen. 2:3). In a series of statements, Jesus predicted the suffering of the Son of Man, based upon what was written in the Old Testament. (See especially Mark 9:12; 14:21, but also 8:31,38; 9:9,31; 10:33; 14:41). The most likely basis for a figure who suffers so as to bring about the reconciliation and redemption of others is found in the suffering servant passages of Isaiah. (Isaiah 49:1-4; 52:13–53:12). This servant sometimes appears to be the nation Israel (Isa. 49:3; 52:14-15), but at other times an individual within the nation (Isa. 49:5; 53:8) who will redeem Israel so Israel in turn can become a redemptive force among the nations. It is not obvious in Isaiah that the servant will be the very Son of God, nevertheless God is apparently especially present in the Servant so that he will "make many righteous, and he shall bear their iniquities" (Isa. 53:11). When Jesus referred to himself as Son of Man, he clearly identified himself as such a servant. "For the Son of Man came not to be served but to serve, and to give his life a ransom for many" (Mark 10:45).

In two other statements Jesus obviously identified the Son of Man with the divine figure in Daniel, who was like a man, but more than a man.

> As I watched in the night visions,
> I saw one like a human being
>   coming with the clouds of heaven.
> And he came to the Ancient One
>   and was presented before him.
> To him was given dominion
>   and glory and kingship,
> that all peoples, nations, and languages
>   should serve him (Dan. 7:13-14).

Jesus clearly drew upon this imagery:

> Jesus said, "I am; and
>   'you will see the Son of Man
> seated at the right hand of the Power,'
>   and 'coming with the clouds of heaven.'"
>                    (Mark 14:62; see also 13:26).

By the phrase "Son of Man" Jesus therefore proclaimed himself the one who is like a human, but more than a human, who is to receive an everlasting kingdom from God. Though Jesus was like a man, he is at the same time actually divine because he was to rule over an everlasting kingdom. By employing "Son of Man" Jesus sought not only to declare his relationship with humankind, but also with God.

We have now scrutinized the grounds by which Mark concluded that Jesus was Son of God and Son of Man. He believed such a decision was warranted because of the actions and explicit statements of Jesus. We turn now to other New Testament writers, specifically John, Matthew, Luke, Paul, and the writer of Hebrews to ascertain additional claims for the unanimous conviction that Jesus came from God.

## *The Word Became Flesh*

The Gospel of John provides the clearest affirmation as to who Jesus is. The Word (*logos*) has been around as long as God. "In the beginning was the Word" (John 1:1). In other words, Jesus is immortal — he has been forever and will forever be. About God, the Psalmist wrote,

> **Before the mountains were brought forth,**
> **or ever you had formed the earth and the world,**
> **from everlasting to everlasting you are God. (Ps. 90:2).**

Jesus too was around before the mountains. He too is from everlasting to everlasting.

But not only was Jesus in the beginning — he was with God. By use of "Word" (*logos*), John clearly has in mind the agency of the Word in speaking into existence all that is. "All things came into being through him, and without him not one thing came into being" (1:3). When God created light, he said, "Let there be light" (Gen. 1:3). God therefore created everything by his Word, and that Word, in John's view, was Jesus. Likewise God created everything through wisdom. Wisdom was beside God "like a master worker" (Prov. 8:30). The outer manifestation of wisdom is the word that contains it. Therefore creation through wisdom is ultimately creation by the Word. John situated Jesus all the way back to God's beginning work in creation. He was around from the very beginning. All things were made through him.

John was not finished. He ended with the awesome, electrifying charge that the Word, that is, Jesus, is God. Since Jesus is everlasting, he obviously has divine characteristics. John puts it, "and the Word was God." Just how John understands the relationship of Jesus and God is not clear. Later he reported Jesus' statement, "The Father and I are one" (John 10:30). Does John envision two deities: the Father, and the Son? Or does he envision a superior deity and a lesser one?

Immediately preceding the last quoted verse Jesus said, "My Father, who has given them to me, is greater than all" (10:29, NIV). Or does John think that Jesus is one of the three manifestations of God? The NRSV translates 10:29 "What my Father has given me is greater than all else." I think the NRSV translation is most representative of John. It seems unlikely that we can fine tune John's views in the manner of the fourth century theologians who hammered out a doctrine of the trinity (for example, the Nicene Creed). It is clear, however, that for John, God is fully realized in Jesus. We can see this in specific developments within the Gospel.

Jesus was sent from God. This is John's favorite terminology in regard to Jesus' identity. [John uses this phrase 18 times, for example, "I have not come on my own. But the one who sent me is true" (John 7:28).] Jesus entered the human arena from another realm. He was relocated onto human turf by God. He is an outsider. But he took on human flesh. "The Word became flesh and lived among us" (John 1:14). John sets out the humanity of Jesus as much as any Gospel. Jesus ate, drank, slept, wept, grew tired, and exhibited many other human characteristics. Even though God, his existence in the flesh was real. It's not as if he just appeared to be human. He was truly God, truly man.

John, or better, Jesus in the Gospel of John had another way of declaring Jesus God. Jesus in the Gospel often employs "I Am" (*ego eimi*) in reference to himself. Often Jesus employed it to declare a role. I am the bread of life (John 6:35,51), the light of the world (John 8:12; 9:5), the door (10:7,9), the shepherd (10:11,14), the resurrection and the life (11:25), the way, the truth, and the life (14:6), and the vine (15:1,5). Sometimes he uses "I am" to indicate that he is the one, for example, when the soldiers and police seek him in the garden (John 18:5). In four instances, however, he clearly used the phrase without further reference. When Moses asked God for his name as he stood facing the burning bush, God answered, "I AM WHO I AM" (in Septuagint, *ego eimi ho on*, Exod. 3:14). In effect then, Jesus identified himself as the I AM who appeared to Moses, that is, God himself.

In John 8:24 told the Pharisees who criticized him, "you will die in your sins unless you believe that I am he." In other words unless people believe that Jesus is identical with the one who appeared at the burning bush, they will die in their sins. In John 8:28 Jesus told the same group, "When you have lifted up the Son of Man, then you will realize that I am he." The Jesus who died on the cross will rise to live again. In the Gospel of John, Jesus laid down his life in order that he himself could take it up. "I have power to lay it down, and I have power to take it up again" (John 10:18). In John 8:56 Jesus declared boldly to the Jews that Abraham rejoiced and was glad that he had seen his day. They chided him for implying that he had seen Abraham. He then put it stronger, "Very truly, I tell you, before Abraham was, I am" (John 8:58). In this statement he declared his existence prior to Abraham, and his identification with God himself. Finally, Jesus stated plainly that one of the twelve sitting at table with him was going to betray him. Jesus declared that he was telling them this in advance so they would recognize his prior knowledge regarding events yet to transpire, that is, the powers of God himself. "I tell you this now, before it occurs, so that when it does occur, you may believe that I am he" (John 13:19).

## *God with Us*

Matthew and Luke agree with John that Jesus was sent from God — that is, he is the Son of God. Unlike John, they offer an explanation for how it is that Jesus is both God and man. He is truly God, truly man since he was conceived by the Holy Spirit in the womb of Mary. "She was found to be with child from the Holy Spirit" (Matt. 1:18; Luke 1:35). The bedrock affirmation which established Jesus' deity for

Matthew and Luke was not so much that he was born of a virgin, though they both reported Mary's virginal status, but that he was conceived by the Holy Spirit. The Holy Spirit conception tells us precisely what we want to know. It tells us that God, the maker of heaven and earth, participated in the conception of Jesus through his Holy Spirit. Jesus was therefore God because he was conceived by God. At the same time he was human because the conception took place in the womb of Mary, and he was born in the normal human fashion. According to Luke he attained manhood by going through the usual stages of human maturation. "And Jesus increased in wisdom and years, and in divine and human favor" (Luke 2:52).

The doctrine offered as a fortress against humanism should be the Holy Spirit conception. The rallying cry early in this century was the doctrine of the virgin birth. That Mary was a virgin when Jesus was conceived establishes the fact that his father was not a human. The Holy Spirit conception is fundamental inasmuch as it tells who his father is, namely God.

If Jesus was not God until his baptism or resurrection then he didn't experience birth or human maturation through adolescence as God. Rather, as deity, he experienced humanity only as a mature person. As God-man he was not one "who in every respect has been tested as we are, yet without sin" (Heb. 4:15). I would suggest that Holy Spirit conception is more compatible with scientific and other biblical affirmations than alternate views, if one would believe that Jesus is divine. It is true that the means through which God accomplished this unprecedented feat is not explained, but I am sure the God in whom I believe could handle that. The claim of Matthew and Luke therefore incorporates in a significant manner the various affirmations about Jesus in the New Testament. No alternate suggestion, as far as I can see, comes close. Through Holy Spirit conception Jesus was truly God, truly man.

Luke declared that the father of Jesus was the Holy Spirit. (1:35; 3:23) At the same time his insights reveal a person, who in all the stages of life, was fully human (Luke 2:52). It does not present a problem to the typical churchgoer that Jesus grew from babyhood, to adolescence, to manhood. Christian art has long depicted the baby Jesus, and Jesus in the temple at twelve. But these same believers do not cope so well with that statement of Luke that Jesus grew in wisdom as well as in stature. I once proposed in a sermon that Jesus, though obviously knowing more about God than others of his age, nevertheless increased in knowledge on the way to adulthood in the manner of typical children. I was reproached afterward by a well-meaning brother who suggested that if Jesus was God, he knew all he was ever to know even as a baby. He implied that my statement was on the verge of denying the deity of Christ. But it was Luke, not I, who proposed that Jesus grew in wisdom. Paul too, suggests that by taking on humanity, Jesus voluntarily limited his divine attributes (Phil. 2:7). Luke apparently believed that Jesus, in taking on manhood, gave up the prerogative of complete divine knowledge. He was truly human; truly divine.

A prince and his entourage made a periodic visit through the realm. In a small, out of the way village, his eyes fell upon a shabbily dressed peasant maiden. After spending hours observing her demeanor and ways with the villagers, he fell hopelessly in love. That night was a sleepless one. As he lay listlessly on his bed he turned over in his mind how he could woo the maiden. She would readily consent to be his wife because of the status and prestige. But the prince was intent on winning her for himself. He therefore concluded that he must approach her incognito. He could, without her knowing he was the prince, send her magnificent gifts. But he sadly concluded that by so doing he would win her for the gifts, rather than for himself. As the rays of dawn raced across the eastern sky he knew what he must do. He must put on the clothes of a peasant and go take up residence in the village. If then he happened to win the love of the maiden, it would be for himself.[1]

## *Born of Woman*

Paul tells us that Jesus, the Son of God, came as a man. "But when the fullness of time had come, God sent his Son, born of woman, born under the law" (Gal. 4:4). God sent his Son into the womb of a woman. Jesus came from God and existed prior to his human birth. At the same time he was human, that is, born of woman. In 1 Corinthians Paul declares, "Yet for us there is one God, the Father, from whom are all things and for whom we exist, and one Lord, Jesus Christ, through whom are all things and through whom we exist" (8:6). The same affirmations are found in Romans. "Sending his own Son in the likeness of sinful flesh, and to deal with sin, he condemned sin in the flesh" (Rom. 8:3). In Colossians Paul declares that Jesus is the image of God, is before all creation, and all things are created by him (1:15,16). Furthermore, "For in him the whole fullness of deity dwells bodily" (2:9). The work of Christ in the world is therefore, at the same time, the work of God. "In Christ God was reconciling the world to himself, not counting their trespasses against them" (2 Cor. 5:19).

In another manner Paul indicated his conviction that Jesus was God, the maker of humankind. Paul often uses the phrase, "The Lord Jesus Christ," or "the Lord Jesus," for example, "The Lord Jesus on the night when he was betrayed . . ." (1 Cor. 11:23). In fact, almost without exception, when Paul

---

[1] This is my version of a story found in: Søren Kierkegaard, *Concluding Unscientific Postscript to the "Philosophical Fragments,"* trans. David F. Swenson, ed. Walter Lowrie (Princeton, NJ: Princeton University Press, 1941).

uses the word "Lord," it is in reference to Jesus. The call for a believer to confess Jesus as Lord upon accepting Jesus as Messiah is found in Romans: "If you confess with your lips that Jesus is Lord and believe in your heart that God raised him from the dead, you will be saved" (Rom. 10:9). The significance of this confession becomes clear when one realizes that the Septuagint translation into Greek of the Hebrew Bible consistently translates the special name for God, that is, Yahweh as *kyrios*. The standard English translation of *kyrios* is "Lord." The generic name for God in Hebrew is *elohim*. According to Exodus 6:2, "God also spoke to Moses and said to him: "I am the *Lord*. I appeared to Abraham, Isaac, and Jacob as God Almighty, but by my name 'The *Lord*' I did not make myself known to them." Most modern English translations consistently translate "Yahweh," God's special name, as *Lord*. Paul, therefore, in constantly declaring Jesus "Lord," identified him with the God of the Old Testament.

Paul nowhere mentions the Holy Spirit conception, or that Mary was a virgin. Some scholars thereby conclude that Paul left the door wide open for alternate christologies, for example, adoptionism. But if we take seriously his statement that God sent his Son, born of a woman, then adoptionism is ruled out. Jesus was already the Son of God prior to his human birth. Paul presupposes the same christology as Matthew, Mark, Luke, and John. All five state or imply that (1) Jesus existed prior to his human birth, (2) entered the world in the womb of Mary, and (3) grew into manhood as other humans. So while Paul does not explicitly advance Holy Spirit conception, such is fully compatible with his recorded statements. Even for Paul, Jesus is truly God, truly man.

## *God Was in Christ*

The universal testimony of the New Testament is that the significance of Jesus lies in who he is, that he is from God.

He is from God in the full sense of the word. He is not merely a messenger whom God selected from among the myriads of heavenly beings to fulfill an earthly assignment. As long as God has been around, Jesus has been around. Whatever God has done, he has brought it to fruition through Jesus. The entry of the Son into human time and space is the entry of God himself into human history. He is the grand finale of the acts of God in this world. The meaning and the future of the world are in his hands. Because of him, human history has turned the corner. His life and his death show finally and irrevocably that God loves his universe, but especially humans made in his image. "God's love was revealed among us in this way: God sent his only Son into the world so that we might live through him" (1 John 4:9).

# Questions for Discussion

1. Who do the early crowds think Jesus is?

2. Why did Jesus call himself "Son of Man"?

3. What does "Son of Man" mean in Psalms, Ezekiel, and Daniel?

4. What is the Old Testament background for Jesus as the Word?

5. What is the predominant way of describing Jesus in the Gospel of John?

6. What did Jesus mean when he called himself, "I Am"?

7. In what way is it possible for Jesus to be divine-human?

8. Is an "adoptionist" understanding possible from a New Testament standpoint?

9. Does the Holy Spirit conception of Jesus make a more significant claim than that he was born of a virgin?

10. Did Paul believe that Jesus was preexistent?

11. What does Paul's use of *kyrios* as a manner of addressing Jesus tell us about his understanding of Jesus?

12. Was Christ's body the same before and after his resurrection?

# 3

# He Was Announced by John the Baptist

*I*n the Gospel of Luke, the birth of Jesus is inextricably tied to that of a kinsman — John the Baptist. If the New Testament is a mosaic on Jesus of Nazareth, how did John get into the picture? Is he an interloper? If so, of what sort? Does he get into the act merely as an historical accident because of his great popularity and tremendous following? Is he noteworthy because some of his followers later transferred their allegiance to Jesus? Or is he included in the story merely because he was a kinsman of Jesus and supported the launching of his public ministry? If he appeared only in Luke it would be one thing, but in fact, he receives more attention in each of the four Gospels than any other person, Jesus and two or three of the twelve excepted. Furthermore, John is mentioned in Peter's major discourse to the household of the Roman army officer Cornelius.

After Acts, John the Baptist is never again mentioned in the New Testament. Why is he so crucial at the beginning of the Christian faith, then drops out completely? With this plethora of questions before us, one from among them is fundamental: why does John the Baptist occupy an inextricable role in the message of the New Testament?

## *Make Straight the Way of the Lord*

It is clear from both the New Testament and Josephus (A.D. 37-100, a Jewish historian) that John the Baptist acquired an impressive following (John 3:25). In addition, the officials of the land were well aware of his acclaim. Herod, the king, upon hearing about the fanfare surrounding Jesus' early ministry, was in great fear that "John, whom I beheaded, has been raised" (Mark 6:16). John was in fact a relative of Jesus. We do not know whether they managed to spend any time together as lads. But none of these factors explain why the Gospel writers felt compelled to bring John into the picture when the story line focused on Jesus.

The most straightforward statement is one which John supplied. It is mentioned by all the Gospel writers. The Jews sent priests and Levites from Jerusalem to ask John how he identified himself. In their view his posture was so unique that he must lay claim to being one of the eschatological figures. John created quite a stir in the countryside. People came from as far as Jerusalem to hear him. John did not immediately volunteer any information. So the priests put questions to him. Are you the Christ? Are you Elijah? Are you the prophet? In each case they received a negative response. Frustrated with nothing to go on, they pleaded, "Who are you? Let us have an answer for those who sent us. What do you say about yourself?" (John 1:22). John finally spoke up, "I am the voice of one crying in the wilderness, 'Make straight the way of the Lord,' as the prophet Isaiah said" (John 1:23). This statement obviously is a key for understanding John. Each of the Gospels quote this Isaianic statement (Matt. 3:3; Mark 1:3; Luke 3:4).

In the first three Gospels, John the Baptist is identified as Elijah, despite his disclaimer in John (1:21). If this poses a problem, we need to remember that in the synoptics it was Jesus who identified John with Elijah, not John himself. From this observation a framework for the rest of the chapter emerges. First, we will notice what John said about himself and the content of his message. Then we will focus on what Jesus said about John.

## *John's Statement about Himself*

When asked to present a job description, why did John quote the verse from Isaiah? First John wanted to root his life and work precisely in the tradition of Israel's prophets. He did not conceive his mission as revolutionary, that is, to overthrow Israel's historical faith. He wished to align himself with the God of Abraham, David, Isaiah, and Jeremiah. "To understand me," John in effect declared, "you have to keep in mind Yahweh, maker of heaven and earth, who has been involved with humankind from the beginning. You have to remember his promises and word as delivered to his prophets from time immemorial. I, John, am fulfilling his promise that at some future date a voice will cry in the wilderness, 'make straight the way of the Lord.' I am that voice." John thus claimed, as his mission and message, the heritage of Yahweh's great prophets.

John modeled his life after that of the prophets of Israel. "Now John wore clothing of camel's hair with a leather belt around his waist, and his food was locusts and wild honey" (Matt. 3:4). The similarities with Elijah are obvious. John lived by himself in wilderness regions, wore skins like Elijah, and ate the same kind of food (2 Kgs. 1:8). Even if John did not seize upon an Elijah role, others did it for him, Jesus among them. To make any sense at all out of John one must locate him in the stream of God's salvific work. In this respect, John and Jesus are the same. New Testament writers hail Jesus' advent as the capstone of history. They do not hermetically seal him off from past and future. They do not disengage him from what went before and after. They situate him precisely in the continuum of God's salvific work on behalf of humankind. Jesus is the one who brings to an apex the mighty works of Israel's God. The Baptist is similarly situated. He is not, however, the culmination of God's work. He is a forerunner — a herald for that culmination. "He himself was not the light, but he came to testify to the light" (John 1:8).

Second, John wished to be identified as an eschatological herald. His role was essential, though not as an end in itself. The Isaiah declaration envisions a servant who travels ahead of an emperor and smoothes over the rough spots in the road so the trip will be as comfortable as possible. He removes rocks and logs. He fills in ruts and ditches. John visualized his efforts as traveling Jesus' route in advance so as to prepare a roadbed suitable for the king. In this role as preparer, John is inextricably intertwined with the ministry of the one for whom he prepared.

John saw his work exclusively as that of a herald. His disciples had great aspirations for their master. They were jealous for his advance. "Rabbi, the one who was with you across the Jordan, to whom you testified, here he is baptizing, and all are going to him" (John 3:26). John felt no pangs of jealousy. After all, he arrived on the scene for that very purpose. He conceived himself as a sign pointing to Jesus. "For this reason my joy has been fulfilled. He must increase, but I must decrease" (John 3:29,30).

The attitude of John is a paradigm for all disciples. If a woman or man should walk with the Lord, Jesus' significance must increase daily. We believers may point acquaintances to the Lord and disciple them in Jesus' ways. But as soon as the disciple gets acquainted with the Lord on his or her own, we must retreat so as to make way for the Lord to move up front, center. He must increase, we must decrease. How many are the times that those who point someone to the Lord keep strings attached for their own self-fulfillment? I have known soul winners who actually felt threatened when those they brought to the Lord stepped out on their own and were no longer dependent. Our task is to prepare the Lord's way, then get out of the road and let them travel on it. That is what John did. "He must increase, I must decrease."

## *Repent and Believe in the Gospel*

We have just put a finger on John's understanding of his mission. What then was his message? The synoptics are unanimous in regard to the basic theme. "The time is fulfilled, and the kingdom of God has come near; repent, and believe in the good news" (Mark 1:14,15). God is about to break into history in a decisive manner. The appropriate action is repentance in anticipation of deliverance.

What if an announcement comes out of Washington that within six months importation of foreign crude will be prohibited, accompanied by an edict that energy consumption shall be cut by one-half. A proclamation of this magnitude would have electric effect on the citizenry. John's declaration caused similar excitement inasmuch as many Palestinians were disgruntled with Roman occupation and Herodian antics. They lived in hope that these oppressive overlords would bite the dust. John's message touched a nerve. Many anxiously awaited what he proclaimed. They constantly searched the horizons, anticipating restoration of the ancient Davidic monarchy in all its power and grandeur.

Not everyone, of course, longed for an inbreaking of God's kingdom or John's particular version of how it would be inaugurated. First, in anticipation of the inbreaking, John called all men and women to repentance — an about face in lifestyle. Those who already claimed to live by God's rules, for example, the Pharisees, were offended. John had his nerve to suggest they were in need of repentance. After all, they had stood in the breech for decades, being God's persons against the inroads of ever-threatening paganism, and Hellenism. But John did not exclude them from repentance's demand. He charged them with arrogance. They claimed exemption on the ground of dedication to the law, its precise interpretation, and their physical descent from Abraham. John challenged them to "Bear fruit worthy of repentance" (Matt. 3:8). He warned them, "I tell you, God is able from these stones to raise up children to Abraham" (Matt. 3:9).

The Pharisees took special umbrage to the fact that he expected them to be baptized. After all, it was they who administered baptism to Gentiles who converted to Judaism. And now comes John, this fierce wilderness preacher, who has the audacity to suggest that they submit to the identical rite demanded of the Gentiles. Even they did not require as radical a life change as John. They believed that the kingdom would arrive the very day each Jew faithfully kept every iota and dot of the law (Matt. 5:18). John charged that the kingdom's arrival is not dependent on man's righteousness or law keeping. When God wants to break into history, he will do so whether his people are ready or not.

John announced that the day of the Lord is on its way. The inbreaking of the kingdom will neither be forced nor impeded by aggressive human activity. The response demanded is repentance and joyful acceptance of the good news of forgiveness. Even we need to accept the fact that when God gets ready to move, he moves. He is not subject to the decisions and actions of well meaning but misguided prophets and healers, or keepers of orthodoxy.

A further insight into John the Baptist's message is provided by Luke. Upon hearing John's fervent call to repentance, his auditors wanted to know the concrete contours of the lifestyle envisioned. If they were to do an about face, what should be the characteristics of the new path? First, the new way is one in which the penitents share what they have with others. They are to share both food and clothing (Luke 3:11). The tax collectors wanted it laid out specifically. What should they do? John did not hesitate. "Collect no more than the amount prescribed for you." The soldiers wondered how repentance applied in their case. John urged them to treat justly the people with whom they dealt. They should neither extort nor force goods, and be content with their wages.

From these concrete responses it is obvious that by a turnabout in life, John envisioned a concern for the needs of others rather than the fulfilling of self-interests. Repentance, therefore, was not from false religious institutions or worship, but from the fallacious assumption that unless one takes care of number one no one else will. John insisted that preparation for the inbreaking of God involves a change of heart about one's fellows. One must keep their welfare in mind as well as one's own.

In all these ways John anticipated the mission and message of Jesus. He pointed people toward Jesus' radical proposal that those in the kingdom of God are under mandate to love even their enemies.

## John and Jesus: A Contrast

The main thrust of John's message pinpointed the coming kingdom and its characteristics. The style and ministry of John may be highlighted further through a contrast with that of Jesus. The basic message of the two was the same. Matthew especially spotlighted the similarity. "From that time Jesus began to proclaim, 'Repent, for the kingdom of heaven has come near.'" (Matt. 4:17).

The baptism of Jesus, however, had additional features. John baptized with water for repentance and forgiveness of sins (Mark 1:4). The one who came after and to whom John pointed, that is, Jesus, baptized with the Holy Spirit and with fire (Matt. 3:11). The baptism of the Holy Spirit is to come upon those who humbly submit to the Lordship of God's messiah. The baptism of fire is for those who refuse his free ticket into the kingdom. It is a baptism of destruction. "His winnowing fork is in his hand, and he will clear his threshing floor and will gather his wheat into the granary; but the chaff he will burn with unquenchable fire" (Matt. 3:12). The vision is taken from Malachi. The day of the Lord will be a time of great rejoicing for those who are ready through repentance and dedication. The wicked, however, will suffer destruction and burning (Mal. 4:1-3).

In addition to the different baptisms other contrasts distinguished the ministries of John and Jesus. John lived in isolated regions. Jesus frequented towns and cities. John lived a Spartan, ascetic existence. Jesus ate and drank whatever his hosts, whether rich or poor, set before him. John and his disciples regularly fasted and practiced other pious acts. Jesus and those who followed him never kept a well-ordered, religious regimen. The major difference, as John delineated it, is that Jesus was uniquely under the auspices of the Spirit. Included among Jesus' works were healing and helping. From the Scripture and elsewhere we hear of John's preaching, but never that he was acclaimed as a miracle worker (John 10:41).

## He Is the Elijah to Come

Jesus had many kind words for John the Baptist. He remembered hearing that before he was born, Mary, his mother, visited Elizabeth, John's mother, when both were with child. They spent the days in wonderment, praising God for their role in his great salvation. He remembered the reports about the auspicious signs surrounding John's birth: how his parents were beyond the age for child bearing,

Zechariah's long months of speechlessness, how Zechariah selected John's name despite strong objection by the relatives, and the portentous utterances pertaining to John's role in God's plans (Luke 1:1-80). Jesus may have closely followed John's career. As far as we know, he himself did not become involved. But he praised John as a man of God. When Jesus wished to "fulfill all righteousness" (Matt. 3:15) by being baptized, he went to John. He wholeheartedly accepted the prospects of receiving John's disciples as his own.

After a period of rising popularity, and impassioned pleading for repentance, John so antagonized the religious and political leaders that they incarcerated him. In prison John began to have second thoughts about Jesus. Was he indeed the one to reestablish the Davidic hegemony? If God was on the verge of changing history, why should he, John, be wasting in prison? He apparently had the mistaken notion, one with which we are too often afflicted, that when God gets around to doing what is exciting and far reaching, we will be where the action is. John felt cut off. He was completely out of it. So John sent his disciples to Jesus with the question, "Are you the one who is to come, or are we to wait for another?" (Matt. 11:3). Jesus didn't say yes; he didn't say no! Instead he paraphrased a statement in Isaiah (61:1-3) which speaks of God's anointed giving sight to the blind, causing the lame to walk, curing the lepers and the deaf, raising the dead, and preaching the good news to the poor (Matt. 11:4-6). Jesus ostensibly identified himself as this servant and accepted the anointed one's (messianic) mission. John's position was a precarious one. He had his charge from God; a mission fraught with danger. He discharged it faithfully. As a result, he wound up in prison. John was supplied privileged information about the future from God, but he was not told all. He had to accept his mission and its outcome in faith that somehow his life would eventually count to the glory of God. John was willing, but anxious.

In his heyday John was something of a regional hero with the people of the land. They admired his fervor, his fierce opposition to the sins of their leaders, and his message of repentance and mercy. They likewise were puzzled at his incarceration. In response to their questions about John, Jesus responded with commendation and adoration. He singled John out as an unbending prophet with a divine message. His demeanor and dress were unlike those of authority or royalty. He aspired only to be God's servant. Jesus lifted him higher than any claim John ever made for himself. "Truly, I tell you, among those born of women no one has arisen greater that John the Baptist." It was his role as a herald for the Son which conferred on John this unrestrained praise. He belonged among the great prophets. He was the greatest of the species. In Jesus' thinking he fulfilled the prediction of Malachi, "Lo, I will send you the prophet Elijah before the great and terrible day of the LORD comes" (Mal. 4:5). So Jesus confided to the crowd, "if you are willing to accept it, he is Elijah who is to come" (Matt. 11:14).

Jesus did not say John was literally Elijah, brought back to earth from heaven. But he asserted that John fulfilled the role prophesied by Malachi. He appeared before the inbreaking of God. He spent his days and nights warning of its immediacy. The eschatological figure, long awaited by those with messianic expectations, had finally arrived. The kingdom, now that Elijah has come, is on the verge of erupting. On a later occasion when Jesus, Peter, James, and John were in retreat on the mountain peak, Moses and Elijah appeared. Jesus withdrew and conversed with them. Then Moses and Elijah disappeared. God himself spoke from heaven and identified Jesus as the new and only voice for this day and age. Moses and Elijah may have commanded attention in the past, but the voice of Jesus only remains. Elijah weighed heavily on the minds of the disciples as they made their way down the mountain. They asked Jesus why the scribes assigned such great importance to Elijah's return prior to the awesome day of the Lord. Jesus answered that the scribes were correct in this emphasis. In fact, John is the predicted Elijah. He is God's messenger, God's servant, despite the strange turn of events in which he was imprisoned and killed. He came as predicted prior to the arrival of the messiah. John's death was not in vain. The prophecy did not fail. The messianic age was now present. The messiah was right before their eyes.

John's rise and fall may in some special way say a word about our contribution to the kingdom. We may fulfill a divinely commissioned mission, but suffer ignominy and defeat. John was not clued in in advance nor given any guarantee as to the outcome of his efforts. Even a prophet of God does not know everything about God's specific plans and ways. All he knows is what God discloses. John did not cast himself in the role of Elijah; Jesus did that. John had doubts along the way as to his accomplishments or whether Jesus was in fact God's messiah. In our anxiety about the uncertainties of life — how little it is we know about the future, how life is so often full of surprises — we need to recall that God's prophets had that precise problem. When we complain that we have no clear vision as to the direction for our next step, since God has withheld privileged information, we should recall that the prophets fared no better. John faced these uncertainties as a man, or better still, God's man! John cast himself in a very humble role, that of a servant preparing the way. He did not even pinpoint his identity in as conspicuous a role as "Elijah." Jesus cast him in that role. If we willingly acknowledge a humble mission as our life's work, God and his Son themselves may amazingly recast it into hallowed importance.

## A Preface to the Gospel

John was in a long line of prophets. He was the last in that line. "For all the prophets and the law prophesied until John came" (Matt. 11:13). With John's death an illustrious dynasty of God's servants came to a close. But despite phasing out the prophetic mission, the work of God continues. What follows is more glorious and rewarding, for John helped usher in a new day — a new kingdom which far surpasses all those preceding it. John reveled in the arrival of the kingdom. He himself was not a part it. "The least in the kingdom of heaven is greater than he" (Matt. 11:11). By these words Jesus at once spoke of John's greatness, and at the same time of the unutterable joys and riches of God's kingdom. Jesus ushered in that kingdom.

John the Baptist is an inextricable rubric in the Gospel of Jesus Christ. He is indispensable because of the one to whom he pointed. He prepared the way. His role makes it clear that a New Testament theology must give recognition to the fact that God always anticipates and prepares. He recruits and employs responsive servants for these tasks. John was not an end in himself. He came to identify and elevate the Son of God. "He must increase, but I must decrease." He has a vital part in the Jesus story line. He anticipates and points out the Son, God's anointed.

# Questions for Discussion

1. Why was John the Baptist important historically?

2. Why did Peter mention John the Baptist in his sermon at Caesarea (Acts 10)?

3. Why is John the Baptist important in the Gospels?

4. Did John the Baptist cast himself in the role of Elijah?

5. Why was Elijah connected with the coming of the Lord in the Old Testament?

6. How did Jesus depict the purpose of John the Baptist?

7. How did John perceive his role as one who prepares the way?

8. In what manner is John's self understanding important for disciples today?

9. What was the focus of John the Baptist's message?

10. How did Luke depict John's message?

11. Did John the Baptist have any of the gifts highlighted in 1 Corinthians?

12. How did John the Baptist's baptism differ from that of Jesus?

# 4
# He Was Anointed by the Holy Spirit

When Jesus was about thirty, the time came to take up God's assigned ministry. It was a ministry of healing and helping, of comforting the afflicted, and afflicting the comfortable. Like John, he too asserted the nearness of the kingdom. Because it was a ministry instigated by God, victories were assured. At the same time manifold perils arose. But God never sends forth his servants without adequate preparation. He did not send Israel immediately to the land promised, but gave them time to get ready, both mentally and physically. "God did not lead them by the way of the land of the Philistines, although that was nearer; for God thought, 'If the people face war, they may change their minds and return to Egypt'" (Exod. 13:17). God's only begotten Son was no exception and neither are we. Sometimes we chafe at the bit, eager to take up the ministries God has assigned. But God knows when we are ready. He sends us to our ministries only when we are mentally and emotionally prepared.

How is God to get his Son ready for ministry? He has
been at work since Jesus' earthly birth. Specific actions, however, get underway as the time draws near. First, through his
Spirit, God led Jesus to the Jordan to be baptized by John.
Second, and this is assigned significance by the fact that all
four Gospel writers report it, upon being baptized in water
God sent his Spirit to empower the Son's ministry. Third,
God affirmed Jesus' Sonship. And fourth, the Spirit led Jesus
into the wilderness to be tempted of the devil. These were the
stages of preparation in the months prior to the actual
launching of the ministry.

In like manner, our own ministry commences with baptism, the coming of the Holy Spirit, being affirmed to sonship, and a rash of temptations and trials. These are bench-
marks for those who preach, but not for them alone. The
ministry of all disciples — that is, all Christians — is inaugurated in precisely the same manner. All disciples have gifts
which empower them for serving the body. These gifts differ
— therefore different ministries (Rom. 12:3-8). But whatever
our ministry, we commence it having been prepared by God,
just as he prepared his only Son.

## He Went Up Immediately from the Water

Baptism preceded Jesus' ministry. Likewise baptism is a
first step in initiating ours. Why is this so? Perhaps the fact
that Jesus requested baptism from John will provide a clue.

Jesus went into the wilderness where John was baptizing
in order to secure his own baptism. Why was John baptizing
those who came to him? John's avowed mission was to prepare women and men for the imminent inbreaking of God's
kingdom. Repentance was demanded. The first concrete
move signaling repentance called for baptism and the confession of sins. "And they were baptized by him in the river
Jordan, confessing their sins" (Matt. 3:6).

So Jesus showed up as had various others to comply with God's demand. John was taken aback! The reasons for which he baptized did not seem pertinent in Jesus' case. Furthermore, the baptism exercised by Jesus, that of the Spirit, in John's opinion moved the recipient a step further along the way to the kingdom of God. And now, lo and behold, Jesus shows up, the anointed from God for whom John is preparing the way, and requests that John baptize him. John couldn't add that all up so he demurred, contending that it made more sense for Jesus to baptize him. Jesus thought otherwise. "Let it be so now; for it is proper for us in this way to fulfill all righteousness" (Matt. 3:15).

Why does Jesus think baptism has something to do with righteousness? Righteousness basically means doing what is right. The right response to the demands of God is obedience. Jesus recommended a responsiveness to God's way that even exceeded that of the Pharisees. "Unless your righteousness exceeds that of the scribes and Pharisees, you will never enter the kingdom of heaven" (Matt. 5:20). In order to enter God's kingdom, his demands must be met. Jesus apparently had in mind then, that he himself must comply with the demands of the kingdom in order to lead people into it. The one who ushered in the kingdom could not himself sidestep the rules. By his own obedience he blazed the trail for others to follow. He identified the right action of the kingdom, not only by talk, but by his own example. For this reason he sought baptism from John in order to fulfill all righteousness.

John made it clear that repentance is not simply a mental decision. It requires plunging headlong into the activities of the kingdom. The initial clue that one is repenting because of the impending kingdom is the confession of sin and baptism for its remission (Mark 1:4). The second clue is a life which exhibits God's righteousness. "Bear fruit worthy of repentance" (Matt. 3:8). Jesus himself acted in compliance with these clues except that he made no confession of sin. The disciple, both ancient and modern, exhibits all these concrete clues of righteousness as groundwork for launching ministry. Just as Jesus' ministry was launched with baptism, so is that of each disciple. Upon entering the kingdom each believer is issued a task or ministry (1 Pet. 4:8-11). When we are baptized as Jesus was baptized, we initiate our ministry as did he.

## The Spirit of God Descending

When Jesus emerged from the waters of the Jordan in which he was immersed, the heavens opened "and he saw the Spirit of God descending like a dove and alighting on him" (Matt. 3:16). The baptism characterizing Jesus' ministry was that of "the Holy Spirit and fire" (Matt. 3:11). In order that Jesus exhibit all the attributes of discipleship, he was empowered by that same Spirit. All the Gospel writers report his Holy Spirit anointment. John in his Gospel does not explicitly report Jesus' water baptism, but he does announce that the Holy Spirit came down and remained on Jesus (John 1:33). The ministry of Jesus was Spirit filled. He was anointed by the Spirit. He was the anointed — the Christ=Messiah.

If one stops to reflect, he is surprised that Jesus' ministry is inaugurated by the falling of the Holy Spirit. Why did Jesus require Holy Spirit empowerment? After all, he was conceived by the Holy Spirit. His whole life and being were therefore Spirit filled. In fact, John declared that the Spirit was given to Jesus without limit. While the Spirit fills the life of the recipient, he also confers special task-oriented gifts so as to launch special ministries. It is by the Spirit that Jesus and we likewise (John 3:5) are born of God. But in addition, the Spirit assigns (Eph. 4:11-15) and opens up (Acts 2:4; 8:15; 10:44) ministries to special groups. The Holy Spirit initiated and empowered Jesus' ministry. Jesus needed Holy Spirit empowerment just as we do. He confronted the indifferent as well as the downright hostile. He was attacked by both men and demons. He met these challenges head on, buoyed up by the Holy Spirit of the Father. Even though as Son, he needed the Spirit's assistance to enable his ministry.

What are the specific ramifications of Jesus' empowerment? First, the Spirit directed Jesus in his days of preparation. Immediately upon baptism, Jesus was led by the Spirit into the wilderness to be tempted by the devil (Luke 4:1). After he successfully resisted the onslaughts of Satan, the Spirit directed him back to Galilee (Luke 4:14). Second, in his inaugural sermon Jesus quoted Isaiah 61:1-3, pinpointing the Spirit anointment as his commissioning for preaching good news to the poor, restoring sight to the blind, and setting at liberty those imprisoned. By quoting Isaiah 61:1, "The spirit of the Lord God is upon me, because the Lord has anointed me," Jesus identified his Holy Spirit anointment and also validated his messiahship.

Jesus understood his first sermon as confirming his Spirit anointment. He preached. He healed the sick and restored life to the dead (Luke 4:25-27). Jesus assigned the identical ministry to his disciples. He "gave them power and authority over all demons and to cure diseases, and he sent them out to proclaim the kingdom of God and to heal" (Luke 9:1,2). He likewise shared these powers with the seventy, who after being sent out, came back "with joy, saying, 'Lord, in your name even the demons submit to us'" (Luke 10:17). The Spirit empowered Jesus to preach and heal, which he in turn conferred on the disciples. As far as we can tell, however, from the Gospel writers, Jesus did not speak in tongues. Jesus rejoiced in the Holy Spirit for his and the disciples' victories (Luke 10:21). The details of Jesus' ministry were fleshed out by the power of God's Spirit. The mighty manifestations of power were not Jesus' own. They were amplifications of the Spirit's work.

Just as Jesus' ministry commenced with his baptism and Holy Spirit anointment, so likewise the ministry of each believer. The ministry of believers in the twentieth century is not exactly identical with that of Jesus. It is not exactly the same as that of the apostles. But the identical spirit of God empowers our ministry. The impressive attribute of Jesus' and the apostolic ministry was the great outpouring of love. It is precisely this same unmitigated love which marks our ministry "because God's love has poured into our hearts through the Holy Spirit that has been given to us" (Rom. 5:5). The Spirit assigns the different ministries to concretize and incarnate the constant love of God (Rom. 12:1-6).

## *This Is My Beloved Son*

Not only did God anoint Jesus with the Spirit, he affirmed him as Son. So awesome were the powers Jesus confronted in inaugurating his ministry that he welcomed all of God's proffered resources. It is not incidental, as Jesus faced the two most demanding phases of his ministry — the launching and the crucifixion — that God affirmed him as the beloved Son with whom he is well pleased. God assigned Jesus the most perilous mission in his whole universe. But he did not send him forth unprepared or unassisted. He ushered in his public proclamation by the anointment of the Spirit. At the same time he made perfectly clear who he is. He is God's own Son. God loves him. He is pleased with the work he came to do.

Jesus' ministry was opposed all the way. First of all, he faced Satan himself (Mark 1:13). Next, he was subjected to the indifference, scorn, and even anger of those who were close to him. His friends thought him demented (Mark 3:21). His mother and brothers were embarrassed (Mark 3:31). His neighbors, who watched him grow up, were offended by his words and deeds (Mark 6:3). The local officials were shaken by the demons who opposed him, and asked him to leave (Mark 5:17). The Pharisees leveled charges of blasphemy and violation of God's laws (Mark 2:7,24). Even his own disciples took a long time to add up two and two. They apparently relished being identified with the frenzy he created wherever he went. But it was more than a year before the light began to dawn as to who he really was (Mark 6:51,52; 8:14-21). It was only toward the end of Jesus' ministry that Peter confessed, "You are the Christ" (8:29). How was God to prepare his Son for such a treacherous and taxing ministry? He made his support explicit. "You are my Son, the Beloved; with you I am well pleased" (Mark 1:11). With this assurance Jesus was affirmed. He was ready to confront head on the impossible foe. Being certified as God's Son assured a head start if not incredible odds.

Once the disciples finally confessed Jesus as God's Messiah, the Son of the living God, a new preparation ensued. The grand and climactic act in Jesus' mission was his death for the sins of the world. In this case too, it was mission impossible. God got Jesus ready. Jesus, in turn, prepared the disciples. "Then he began to teach them that the Son of man must undergo great suffering, and be rejected by the elders, the chief priests, and the scribes, and be killed" (Mark 8:31). Jesus faced opposition, not only to his giving, loving activities, but also to the sacrificial purpose of his death. It was completely foreign to Peter's mindset that the Messiah, once arrived, would die. "Peter took him aside, and began to rebuke him" (Mark 8:32). Death was no piece of cake for Jesus either. As it drew near, he grew increasingly anxious and finally was torn up inside. "I am deeply grieved, even to death" (Mark 14:34). At one point he begged God to abort that phase of the mission. "Remove this cup from me" (Mark 14:36). On the cross he felt completely alone and abandoned. "My God, my God, why have you forsaken me?" (Mark 15:34). But despite the anxiety and despair, he was willing to abide by the decision of the Father. "Yet not what I want, but what you want" (Mark 14:36).

How did God prepare and support his Son in such a humiliating, threatening, and excruciating death? Despite the deep and prolonged anguish, Jesus persevered. God fortified him for a catastrophic end by affirming his Sonship a second time. The three inner-circle disciples — Peter, James, and John, climbed a mountain which towered above the surrounding terrain. There Moses and Elijah, powerful and acclaimed leaders from Israel's past, appeared and conversed with Jesus. After a lengthy discussion they disappeared, leaving Jesus alone. In the hearing of the three, God exalted Jesus above Moses and Elijah. He was positioned head and shoulders above the most highly respected religious figures of the past. God spoke clearly and distinctly so that those who heard could never doubt. "This is my Son, the Beloved; listen to him!" (Mark 9:7). With this assurance, Jesus was affirmed. God knew how traumatic his death would be. He did not leave the Son without a word of support. Now a second time, in his electric and inimitable voice, God affirmed Jesus as Son and promised a love which knows no termination. Now the Son was affirmed psychically and mentally for demons or men.

We know what it means to be affirmed. It supplies the boldness to venture forth on uncharted courses and defy impossible obstructions.

Dorothy and I left Boston and Miami for São Paulo, Brazil, then on to Buenos Aires, Argentina, in the summer of 1979. I taught a graduate course in each city, and Dorothy spent numerous hours sharing with missionary wives. We left Abilene in May. I worked on a book in Massachusetts in June and July. I wrote Bryan Bost in São Paulo suggesting that he or someone else meet us in Rio de Janeiro to assist us in touring the city for two days. He wrote reporting that two secretaries from São Paulo would meet our plane. But we left Boston before his letter arrived. After the long overnight flight from Miami, we arrived and proceeded through Rio customs with great dispatch. I told Dorothy we should stand around and look conspicuous just in case someone did come to meet us. But Dorothy prefers not to look conspicuous. We took a taxi to the Hotel Canada on the Copacabana. According to our printed travel guide, certain clerks there spoke English. We had a small manual on conversational Portuguese but that was the extent of our acquaintance with the language.

To that point Dorothy had never felt comfortable in a foreign land where the language was other than English. In addition, she experienced considerable anxiety over flying. All of this persisted despite the fact that her husband had visited numerous foreign cities and was exhilarated by the challenge of conquering new ways and customs. Fortunately, the travel guide was detailed and excellent. We made the day without a hitch, managing to visit shops, the beach, and restaurants. We purchased and ordered what we desired all with a limited repertoire of Portuguese. That night upon arriving at the hotel, Dorothy confided that at first she was very nervous. But as the day wore on, she became more relaxed, and actually commenced enjoying the challenge. She said as the result of that day's experience, she was prepared to go with me anywhere. Was I affirmed! I was ready to take on Afghanistan, Iran, Lebanon, you name it!

So God affirmed his Son. He too was fortified for the momentous task ahead. He went forth knowing that God stood behind the shame and trauma. God affirms our sonship. When we are baptized and receive his Spirit, we are now set for the ministry he confers. He prepares us for the tremendous obstacles by affirming our sonship. We are born from above! (John 1:13). We are the sons and daughters of God. "Beloved, we are God's children now" (1 John 3:2). "But to all who received him, who believed in his name, he gave power to become children of God" (John 1:12). Because we are confirmed as his children, we are ready to tackle whatever tasks lie on the road ahead. What a reassurance to be affirmed by God! We are now eager to take up the challenge of his ministry on the college campus, in the inner city, or in the third world. By calling us sons, God provides the courage for any task! We know whose we are. We know that he will be with us to the end of the age.

## Tempted by the Devil

The opposing forces faced by those involved in God's ministry are often flesh and blood. But in addition, we face "authorities . . . powers . . . the spiritual forces of evil in the heavenly places" (Eph. 6:12). When one enters upon ministry, he is bombarded from all sides. The danger is that one will drop out and revert to the ways of the world. The prevarications of the tempter must be withstood. One must turn his back on the whispered suggestion that going with God entails a glory road in which every whim and need is immediately forthcoming. The glory road of the tempter is a perverted one. It is the glory road of human acclaim. It is not the way of God and his Son. "If any want to become my followers, let them deny themselves and take up their cross and follow me" (Mark 8:34). As God readied Jesus for ministry, the tempter vividly placed the alternatives before him. Jesus was explicitly wooed by the Evil One to travel the easy road of human acclaim rather than the thorn infested path of service.

Jesus faced three specific temptations. First, he was encouraged to succumb to hunger pangs — the strong demands of the flesh. Jesus fasted forty days. He was hungry and emaciated. The Devil encouraged giving in to the need for nourishment. Every cell in Jesus' body cried out. He responded to Satan, not by denying the urgency, but countering that certain commitments take priority over the physical, however compelling the need. "One does not live by bread alone, but by every word that comes from the mouth of God" (Matt. 4:4).

The Devil's second allurement taunted Jesus' Sonship. He took Jesus to Jerusalem and situated him on the highest point of the temple. Then he dared him, if he really is the Son of God, to leap off. If indeed he is the Son, no harm will come. If he refuses, he casts doubt on his God connection. Jesus withstood the dare. Sonship does not demand reckless-ness. "Do not put the Lord your God to the test" (Matt. 4:7).

In the third temptation Satan offered to turn over all the kingdoms of the world to Jesus' rule. Many a man has given his heart and soul to reign over a much smaller territory. The temptation was obviously great, but the purchase incredible. To receive rule over these vast domains Jesus had to fall down and worship Satan. Jesus knew his ministry would be a vale of tears. It would take him over many a rocky road. But the alternative — the worship of Satan — was disastrous. "Away with you, Satan! for it is written, 'Worship the Lord your God, and serve only him'" (Matt. 4:10).

All three of Satan's temptations involved serving self, not God. Upon resisting these self demands Jesus was forti-fied for God's ministry. He now had experienced his own power to resist. He was ready to go the way of God — the path of humble serving, the avenue of caring and loving, the way of the cross. He was the Son, prepared by God himself through baptism, the anointment of the Spirit, being affirmed Son, and facing the tempter.

We are likewise readied by God as he initiates ministry through us. We too immediately stand face to face with the tempter. Before we turned to the Lord, we spent our moments and days seeking self-fulfillment, moving in what-ever directions our hearts desired. We quickly responded to all the dares, and received whatever gifts were forthcoming. These enticements did not immediately disappear once we accepted the Lordship of Christ. In fact, for a time they intensified. Satan is not quick to toss in the towel. He had the audacity even to confront the Son of God himself. He holds on to his servants as long as he is able. He whispers in our ears that the demands of God are nitpicky and foolish. Where will it get us in the end to be giving rather than self seeking? A life of giving rather than taking is pure nonsense. If we don't look out for number one, who will? Early in our days with God we find ourselves in a quandary. We are torn between the old demands and God's new ones. God decisively holds before us the options in the report on Jesus' temptations. The way Jesus came out is clearly the way we are to go. In the resistance of the Son there is no question about what we must resist. In these temptations the enticements of Satan are revealed.

Because Jesus withstood, we are encouraged to follow suit. We too are sons. Our Father gets us ready for ministry in the same manner as he did his only Son. He strengthens us for the road ahead. He does not overwhelm or set out tasks before we can handle them. "God is faithful, and he will not let you be tested beyond your strength" (1 Cor. 10:13).

# Questions for Discussion

1. If Jesus was conceived by the Spirit, why did God anoint him with the Spirit?

2. What are the steps in Jesus' preparation for ministry?

3. Are these steps similar to ours?

4. Why did Jesus present himself to John the Baptist for baptism?

5. Did Jesus speak in tongues?

6. Can a church obtain unusual gifts of the Spirit through its own efforts?

7. Why was it important for God to affirm Jesus as his only Son?

8. Are we declared to be children of God?

9. Can we anticipate that our ministry will be opposed as was Jesus'?

10. How did God prepare Jesus for his death?

11. Are we, too, tempted with the three temptations of Jesus?

12. How are we "ordained" to ministry?

# 5
# He Went About Doing Good

*J*esus made an impression on people both because of what he did and what he said. It is difficult to highlight one over the other. Mark emphasized what Jesus did. Matthew, in contrast, gave Jesus' sayings top billing. Peter in the Cornelius household sermon mentions both as keys for unlocking Jesus' charisma and attraction. Jesus astounded people, not simply by his words, but also by his deeds. So Peter reported

> how God anointed Jesus of Nazareth with the Holy Spirit and with power; how he went about doing good and healing all who were oppressed by the devil, for God was with him (Acts 10:38).

It is important theologically to observe that Jesus was a person of both word and deed. It shows that he was not principally an intellectual, nor, on the other hand, a man of affairs — a pragmatist. The style of his life recommends a balance — a life in which word and deed entwine, creating a larger integrated configuration of thought and action. But even more important is the fact that in Jesus the words and actions convey the same message. Unlike many, his life is where his mouth is.

What is there about Jesus' behavior? If one scrutinizes him for a long time, what do his actions convey? If one contemplates the whole of Jesus' life from birth to death, what shines through as the reason for his action? The answer varies in the New Testament from author to author, often in emphasis, and according to the people and concerns addressed. But from these divergent interests we detect an emerging mosaic. The actions of Jesus are addressed to multiple fronts, but certain repeated interpretative declarations provide a theological perspective. One is reminded of John's statement at the close of his Gospel. "But there are also many other things that Jesus did; if every one of them were written down, I suppose that the world itself could not contain the books that would be written" (John 21:25).

The interruption of Jesus' travel through the small Galilean town of Nain depicts the core message radiating from Jesus' deeds. On the way into the village Jesus met a funeral procession. The only son of a widow had died. He was her only visible means of support. Jesus' heart went out (Luke 7:13). He told the young man to get up. Jesus then led him to his mother. The townspeople were overawed. But upon recovering from this numinous turn of events they recognized the hand of God. They praised him! Excitedly they declared "A great prophet has appeared among us. God has come to help his people" (Luke 7:16, NIV).

Why did these people locate God in this event? Was it because of the extraordinary manifestation of inexplicable life-giving power? Perhaps. What they noticed, however, was the compassion and care exhibited by the deed. Had Jesus simply wished to demonstrate sheer, raw power, he could have raised an impressive public figure, the magistrate of a city. But he restored life to the son of a needy, nameless widow. The God of Israel is like that. He moves where people hurt regardless of their status. The people were overwhelmed by the love shining through the deed. For them that pointed to the caring master of the universe. The message from the work of Jesus is that God cares. His steadfast love is concretely transparent to the inhabitants of Nain. It is forever!

## Teaching and Healing: Matthew

Matthew sums up Jesus' ministry: "Jesus went throughout Galilee, teaching in their synagogues and proclaiming the good news of the kingdom and curing every disease and every sickness among the people" (Matt. 4:23). By his words and works Jesus, in Matthew's presentation, ushered in the kingdom of God. "But if it is by the Spirit of God that I cast out demons, then the kingdom of God has come to you" (Matt. 12:28). The mission of Jesus in Matthew is in digging and pouring the foundations for the kingdom of God. Jesus' teaching was indispensable. What he did was decisive. Jesus is Emmanuel, "God with us" (Matt. 1:23).

Jesus is the heavenly king, the recipient of gifts and obeisance (Matt. 2:10,11). He ushers in a kingdom. He presents a sermon which explicates the rules of the kingdom (Matt. 5–7). The kingdom is new and different. Because of its king it will be for "the people who sat in darkness . . . a great light; and for those who sat in the region and shadow of death light has dawned" (4:16). Jesus shares that light with his disciples. "You are the light of the world. . . . Let your light shine before others, so that they may see your good works and give glory to your Father in heaven" (5:14,16). The kingdom's rays fan out from Jesus through the disciples, and from them to every man and woman. "Go therefore and make disciples of all nations" (Matt. 28:19). Jesus guaranteed the increasing radiance of the kingdom's rays through his presence. "And remember, I am with you always, to the end of the age" (Matt. 28:20).

As Matthew opened his Gospel (1:21–4:16) he identified Jesus as the Messiah, that is, the king anointed to shepherd God's people. He was descended from kings, specifically Abraham and David (1:1). It is no accident that in 1:1 David is mentioned before Abraham even though the order is reversed in the succeeding chronology. Herod, the reigning king, angered by the threat of a contender, ordered cruel and inhuman slaughter of all male Jewish babies (2:16). But even the dragnet of Herod failed to ensnare God's anointed. Jesus launched a kingdom — the incomparable kingdom of heaven.

In the second large section of the Gospel (4:17–16:20) Matthew depicts the nature of the kingdom. The kingdom is inaugurated through what Jesus said and did. Matthew first presented the teachings, the guidelines of the kingdom. He followed with accounts of the mighty deeds of the kingdom. The miracles confirm and sustain the teachings. The healings and powerful works authenticate God's involvement. The kingdom is his. All the signs of word and deed point to him. What Jesus did in this middle part of Matthew is crucial for interpreting the purpose of Jesus' works. These will be developed shortly.

The last section (16:21–28:20), sets forth the events which lead to the death and resurrection of Jesus, thereby securing and empowering the kingdom. The kingdom of God is unique. It is a kingdom of love (Matt. 5:43-48). David eked out his kingdom blow by blow through shrewd guerrilla combat. Solomon consolidated the successes of David through calculated alliances and marriages. The mighty empire of Alexander the Great stretched across three continents, secured by superior marching armies and impeccable organizing skills. But the kingdom God inaugurated through Jesus pushed its way outward demonstrating love, giving, and servanthood (Matt. 20:28). The ultimate exhibit of the kingdom's love empowerment came about in the death of the Son of God on a Roman cross located at the rubbish heap of Jerusalem. His blood was poured out for the sins of the world. The crucifixion in this manner became the cornerstone of the kingdom.

There are five major blocks of teaching in the center of Matthew (5:1–26:2), each ending with some version of the phrase "When Jesus had finished saying these things" (Matt. 7:28; 11:1; 13:53; 19:1; 26:1). These may be intentional, imitating the fivefold divisions of the Torah (the Pentateuch) in the Old Testament. These five discourses are each followed by a section depicting Jesus' mighty works. The discourses themselves discuss (1) the ways and rules of the kingdom (the sermon on the mount), 5:1–7:28, (2) the discipline and demands for discipleship in the kingdom, 10:1–11:1, (3) parables and reflections on the growth of the kingdom, 13:1-51, (4) the characteristics of the kingdom, 18:1–19:2, and (5) the end of the age and the consummation of the kingdom, 24:1–26:2.

After each discourse Matthew relates several incidents in which Jesus showed the loving and serving nature of God. The sequence — the words, followed by the works — shows that Matthew wished to make obvious that Jesus confirmed his message through his works. What is the core message of the discourses? How do the deeds of Jesus confirm it? In the heart of the sermon on the mount Jesus declares the ever-watchful care of God for those who seek first his kingly sway, and the similar care and love those who are citizens of the kingdom have for each other. Emulating the example and tutelage of Jesus, his followers are humble, meek, and merciful. Their concern and love for others extend even to their enemies (5:44). The mighty deeds of Jesus confirmed his statements about God's caring, loving nature. By helping and healing, Jesus immediately demonstrated that God is concerned with hurts, pains, and the diseases of his children, of man made in his image.

In Matthew 8 and 9 we assess the people involved, the nature of their circumstances, and Jesus' response. The people who came were from all social classes, occupations of all sorts, men and women alike of all age levels with multifold racial characteristics and religious affiliations. Their problems ranged from excruciating physical pain to deformities to mental anguish. In responding to these variegated and motley mixtures of humanity Jesus demonstrated, as he declared in his discourses, that men and women are more valuable than birds of the air (6:26). The kingdom of God is about his unyielding care, both in word and action.

Jesus healed a leper (8:1-4), a Roman centurion's paralyzed servant (notice the centurion was a Gentile, 8:5-13), and Peter's fevered mother-in-law (8:14,15). Then, as the day came to a close, he handled one by one the needs of persons too numerous to specify. He cast out demons and healed the sick (8:16). He calmed the great storm on the sea (8:23-27). He confirmed his previous charge, "Therefore I tell you, do not worry about your life" (6:25). Then he healed two demoniacs — men, others could not touch — followed by a paralytic (9:1-8). Among those craving the touch of God were the powerful and the powerless, the well-to-do and the indigent, the religious elite and the outcasts. Jesus rubbed shoulders with them all. Jesus' Father is that sort of God. By his action Jesus placarded his Father in bold relief as a God of compassion.

Jesus, to the Pharisees' chagrin, even ate with tax collectors and sinners (9:10-13). Through doing so he emphasized that God is merciful and expects the same of his children. He restored life to the young daughter of a Jewish ruler (9:18-31), and healed a woman, at one time apparently of considerable means before exhausting her resources on various treatments (9:19-22).

Why did Jesus do all these helpful, extraordinary things? On Jesus' own account the kingdom of God is the manifestation of God's watchful, concerned action on behalf of hurting, sensitive people. By what Jesus did, he demonstrated that God loves every man and woman. God is no respecter of persons. As Matthew brought to a close this section of extraordinary deeds he reflected on Jesus' motivation. "When he saw the crowds, he had compassion on them, because they were harassed and helpless, like sheep without a shepherd" (9:36). Unlike many a person of renown the actions of Jesus were not self-serving. He was in no sense an Evel Knievel of the 1960s, who, after cracking his ribs in a famous motorcycle jump over an Idaho canyon hurt all the way to the bank. He had already turned his back on self-aggrandizement in facing Satan in the wilderness. He did nothing to feather his own nest. "Foxes have holes, and birds of the air have nests; but the Son of Man has nowhere to lay his head" (8:20). Jesus came to help people. "Just as the Son of Man came not to be served but to serve, and to give his life a ransom for many" (20:28). Other kingdoms may thrive on getting. God's kingdom survives through giving.

For forty years in a certain city, Christians have supported a Christian Service Center so as to lend a helping hand to all comers. Not only is money available, but clothes, furniture, advice, assistance, and medical, dental, and legal services of various sorts. In a recent month 316 appointments representing 1,165 persons transpired at the Center. To implement the program 125 volunteers gave 1,010 hours of caring service. The volunteers were retirees, housewives, dentists, doctors, even teenagers. These men and women are committed to realizing God's kingdom of love. The activities of God's people sustain his kingdom just as does the proclaiming of his mercy and love. Jesus founded the kingdom of God both by what he said and did.

## The Way of the Cross

We turn now to the Gospel of Mark. Mark had a different audience in mind for his Gospel. Matthew wrote for Jewish Christians who probably lived around Antioch. Mark kept before him the Christians in Rome and therefore, by majority, Romans or Hellenistic transplants. It is the Gospel of Peter as told to Mark. (For Peter's connection with Mark see 1 Peter 5:13. The cryptic "Babylon" probably refers to Rome.) Matthew sought to persuade Jews that Jesus was the long awaited Messiah-king. Mark, addressing Gentiles without these interests, mustered materials to convince his readers that Jesus is the Christ, the Son of God (Mark 1:1). The focus is on Sonship. Jesus as Son exhibits the loving, caring characteristics of his father. He radiates the compassion of God and voluntarily enters into servanthood. As compared with Matthew, Mark tells us little about what Jesus said. The actions of Jesus and their ramifications are his concerns.

The Gospel of Mark is divided into two basic parts. The first half (1:12–8:30) shows the difficulty with which people came to believe that Jesus is the Son of God. The second half (8:31–16:20) shows the difficulty with which those who confessed Jesus as Messiah came to accept the servant messiahship of Jesus. The actions or deeds of Jesus play a key role in each half of the Gospel. In the first, the deeds call to mind the actions of God himself on behalf of Israel, thereby identifying Jesus with God. In the second, the nature of the deeds highlight the loving characteristics of Israel's God. Jesus' works are self-giving and without fanfare. If Jesus is Son, his actions point to a giving, compassionate, caring God. Like father, like son.

In chapter two we enumerated detractors of Jesus' ministry. They simply could not believe in or come to terms with his messiahship. Included are scribes, Pharisees, friends, family, and residents of the region. All of them failed to discern the work of God in Jesus' extraordinary actions. The disciples themselves had the same problem at first. They were with Jesus constantly. They should have put two and two together and recognized the power of God in the stilling of the storm (4:35-41) and the sea (6:47-52), and the feeding of the 5,000 (6:30-44) then the 4,000 (8:1-13).

Mark takes special pains to highlight the difficulty with which even the disciples came to faith. After Jesus calmed the storm, "they were utterly astounded, for they did not understand about the loaves, but their hearts were hardened" (6:51,52). Even after participating in the meal for 4,000 they were still oblivious. Jesus charged them with having eaten the leaven of the Pharisees and Herod (8:15), implying that both they and the disciples supplied natural explanations for these divine happenings. He asked them, "Do you still not understand?" (8:21).

What is it that the disciples are to understand? First, in regard to the storm they should have recalled that when God created wind and sea he spoke them into existence. Jesus was able by a word to still both. One should therefore conclude that his powers were identical with those of God. Then as they observed multitudes eating in the wilderness, one might expect them to call to mind that in an earlier wilderness God himself supplied bread from heaven, that is, manna. How could they fail but locate in these actions the hand of God? But they were slow to depart from commonplace beliefs about God's presence.

It was long in coming — perhaps above two years. But finally the extraordinary acts began to add up. The conclusion was mind boggling. It just had to be that God was empowering Jesus' unusual accomplishments. Peter verbalized the conclusion for the rest. "You are the Christ" (8:29). That confession did not come quickly or easily. It was a great day when the disciples believed.

That was the first step. The next challenge for Jesus was to convince them that messiahship is servanthood. The disciples, like many of us, thought that should God really put in an appearance on earth, he would throw his weight around and exercise clout at every opportunity. Why be God, if people don't suddenly turn to gelatin in your presence and kowtow to your every whim and wish? But a God of that sort is not the father of our Lord Jesus Christ. He prefers to work behind the scenes, even taking up the path of suffering and defeat. Immediately upon Peter's confession, Jesus declared that the Son of man must suffer and be killed. That was more than Peter could handle, at least right then. "Peter took him aside and began to rebuke him" (8:32). At that point Peter could not fathom a divine, suffering servant. But then his thinking was still informed by human presuppositions, if not demonic ones. "Get behind me, Satan!" Jesus said to him, "For you are setting your mind not on divine things but on human things" (8:33).

The reason the Pharisees and Jesus' hometowners missed the God dimension was that by human criteria it just didn't add up. Herod, the Pharisees, and the citizens of Capernaum would have been impressed had Jesus forced his way into their presence, ordered, if not kicked them about, and established himself at the apex of a line of authority. God in their mind had that power and desire. But they simply couldn't picture a penniless God, dwelling among peasants, powerless through poverty, responding to the needs of poor and rich alike, encouraging the merciful and sidestepping acclaim. They could not make any sense at all of the fact that Jesus silenced those he helped (1:43; 5:41; 8:30).

The God revealed in Jesus is for Mark a God of compassion who suffers along with and for humankind. The deeds of Jesus point to his divinity, but only indirectly. Because of what Jesus did and the way in which he did it, it is clear that Jesus' primary concern is that people see the compassion of God in his actions and only then be awed by the power. Had he been chiefly concerned with exhibiting extraordinary power he could have selected more decisive channels. For example, he could have called a press conference at the tomb of David and restored to life that hero king who had been dead a thousand years. Instead, he raised the daughter of Jairus, a man of only local acclaim, a ruler in the synagogue

(5:22). He sensed the deep distress of her parents and hurt with them.

Jesus did what he did because his heart was touched. He pitied the leper (1:41). He anticipated the emptiness of the common people who longed for credible leaders and heroes (8:2,3). The ways of God are loving and caring. By going about doing good Jesus showed that God is not out to dazzle and awe, but to share life intimately and compassionately. The works of Jesus in Mark are not first of all to prove his divinity, but to set forth the sort of deity he and his Father are. It is in the caring nature of the miracles that Jesus is established as Son of the God of the universe, finally and irrevocably. His miracles recommend service, not a display of the spectacular. "For the Son of Man came not to be served but to serve, and to give his life a ransom for many" (Mark 10:45). Jesus' life as well as his death was the way of the cross. The disciple is charged to walk the same path. That is what the miracles mean. "If any want to become my followers, let them deny themselves and take up their cross and follow me" (Mark 8:34).

## *Bring Good News to the Poor and Recovery of Sight to the Blind.*

Luke was author both of a Gospel and a history of the early church. He no doubt saw them as parts one and two of his effort to account for the multiplying communities of Christian faith throughout the Roman empire (Luke 1:1; Acts 1:1-5). Through the Spirit and the Son, God has initiated and will continue to plant communities of salvation to the ends of the earth. [We will discuss the structure of Luke-Acts in more detail in the chapter on the Holy Spirit for which structure is crucial in discerning Luke's views.] In addition to the manifestation of God's power and salvation, Luke believed that people were attracted by the sharing, caring actions of Jesus, his disciples, and the snowballing myriads of believers. The action of Jesus means that God has come to help his people and release them from pernicious entanglements so they are freed to help one another.

Luke, reversing the order of Matthew, suggests that the prior compassionate action of Jesus is the ground upon which he is to be heard and believed. Act first, he implies, then speech has force. As Matthew set it out, Jesus spoke, then authenticated words by action. It is only Luke who reports that prior to calling Peter, James, and John, Jesus captured their attention through net-breaking catches of fish (5:1-7). With their boats about to sink from the sheer weight, the fishermen were astounded since prior to Jesus' arrival they had caught nothing. So Peter fell at the knees of Jesus and exclaimed, "Go away from me, Lord, for I am a sinful man!" Upon catching their attention, and supplying their need, only then did Jesus issue the call to discipleship. The action came first, then the words. The outcome was that three fishermen left their nets and followed him. "Do not be afraid; from now on you will be catching people" (5:10).

Luke was strong on action. He believed that deeds clear the path for hearing. Action is the foundation of credibility. A person's words and deeds should relay one and the same message. Luke included accounts of Jesus helping women and men of every nationality, including even Samaritans (17:11-19), and at every level of society. But more than any of the other Gospel writers, he selected materials emphasizing Jesus' compassion toward women and the poor.

In his opening remarks on the events leading to the birth of Jesus, Luke dwelt on the responses of the women, of Elizabeth and Mary. Even a prophetess named Anna got into the act (2:36-38). We probably think of Jesus as traveling about the countryside accompanied by twelve men. Luke tells us that women also were in the entourage, including Mary Magdalene, Joanna, Susanna, and several others. Among them were women of status and affluence who "provided for them out of their resources" (8:3). Jesus carried on long conversations with Martha and Mary, and listened to and responded to their views on life (10:38-40). It was a woman who pushed through the crowd just in order to touch Jesus and who ended up receiving commendation and healing (8:43). Another woman, crippled and bent for eighteen years, likewise experienced the exhilaration of release (13:10-17). Luke is the only Gospel writer who reported the latter. The women who remained at the cross exceeded the men in courage, keeping watch over Jesus as he faced ignominious death (23:49). These women were firsthand witnesses to the resurrection. They played a later role in the spread of the kingdom. They were among those who repeated over and over the amazing story of the empty tomb, and their later conversations with the resurrected Lord (Acts 13:30,31).

Luke, along with the other Gospel writers, saw in Jesus the care and compassion of God. He is that sort of God. Jesus spoke out and acted on behalf of the downtrodden, the humble and the powerless. He conveyed by his actions that he is the Son of an identical God. Because of his compassion for men and women, rich and poor, Jew and Gentile alike, he inaugurated a church of love and compassion. The result was that churches sprang up like mushrooms throughout the empire (Acts 2ff). The miracles of Jesus established his Sonship in the mode of servanthood, as an outreach to those often ignored and despised.

## *Jesus Did Many Other Signs*

John was as cognizant of the love of God radiating through the actions of Jesus as any of the other Gospel writers. Only he exclaimed, "For God so loved the world that he gave his only Son, so that everyone who believes in him may not perish but may have eternal life" (John 3:16). Only he recorded, "I give you a new commandment, that you love one another. Just as I have loved you, you also should love one another" (13:34). But though he knew the love of God in a special way, he focused on Jesus' miraculous deeds designated "signs." These signs point to the conclusion that Jesus came from God.

> Now Jesus did many other signs in the presence of his disciples, which are not written in this book. But these are written so that you may come to believe that Jesus is the Messiah, the Son of God, and that through believing you may have life in his name (20:30,31).

In his most repeated Christological affirmation, John identified Jesus as the one sent from God.

Early in his Gospel, John explicitly identified two signs which transpired in Galilee: the water changed to wine (2:11) and the healing of the official's deathly ill son (4:54). The identification of these signs has given rise to scholars' locating a book of signs in the Gospel. A typical outline of the Gospel is:

1. Prologue: Jesus the Son sent from God (1:1-18)

2. The Book of Signs: that Jesus was sent from God (1:19–12:50)

3. The Book of Glory: Death and Resurrection (13:1–20:31)

4. Epilogue: Final charge before returning to God (21:1-25)

The heart of the Gospel turns out to be the book of signs as one may already have suspected from 20:30 which serves as a purpose statement for the Gospel. John's theology concerning the works of Jesus is developed, for the most part, in the book of the signs.

Several scholars commence from the two numbered signs early in the Gospel and count Jesus' remaining specific miracles. It turns out that these total seven unless one continues to chapter 21 and counts the 153-fish catch. The significance of seven to biblical accounts has not eluded the scholars, for example, seven clean animals were taken into the ark, Naaman dipped in the Jordan seven times, and letters were addressed to seven churches of Asia. A consensus persists, therefore, that John intentionally set forth a catalogue of seven miracles as follows:

1. The water turned to wine — 2:11
2. The official's son healed — 4:54
3. The thirty-eight-year-old paralytic cured at the pool — 5:9
4. The feeding of the 5,000 — 6:11
5. Jesus walking on the sea of Galilee — 6:19
6. Restoring sight to the man blind from birth — 9:7
7. The raising of Lazarus — 11:44

Despite the suggestiveness of this proposal, the interest of the author apparently lies not in establishing a catalogue of signs but in highlighting the fact that the first two signs occurred in Cana. He is aware of many signs which go unspecified, especially in Jerusalem (2:23; 6:2). The significance of the author's interest in Cana is not immediately apparent unless Nathaniel has special significance to the people for whom he writes. [See the connection of Nathaniel with Cana, 21:2. Only John refers to Nathaniel, though it is commonly assumed that he is identified as Bartholomew in the synoptics.] Regardless of how we perceive John's catalogue of signs, the signs are the route through which men and women come to the conviction that Jesus is the Christ, the Son of God. Furthermore, the most important sign in the Gospel is the resurrection of Jesus Christ which does not make most lists of the seven.

How does John perceive the signs functioning on the path to faith? Perhaps the first sign will provide clues. When Jesus turned the water into wine, John says he manifested his glory

(2:11). What does this mean? In the Gospel, the glory of Jesus is his relationship with and mission from the Father. The water-wine episode thus points to the glory of Jesus, that is, that he is God. (1:1; see also 1:14 where glory is identified with deity.) The disciples, privy to Jesus' role in the sudden appearance of the superior wine, concluded that the deed exceeded human capacities. Only God could pull off such a feat. The result was that the disciples "put their faith in him" (2:11).

John conceived a sign, not as a reality in itself, but as pointing to reality. The reality is that toward which the wine points, that the one who changed the water is from God. Not everyone, however, is concerned to locate the reality to which the sign points. A crowd was involved in the sign — the multiplying of the loaves and fishes. They had their own explanation. They did not recognize anything unusual. Jesus said to them, "You are looking for me, not because you saw signs, but because you ate your fill of the loaves" (6:26). They ate the sign, but didn't see it. They had no inclination to identify the reality to which the sign pointed. The reality to which the unusual supply of food pointed was the God who rained down manna from heaven. The crowd did not connect their event with that one. They were oblivious to the reality. The reality is that Jesus came from God. It is that to which the sign points. "This is the work of God, that you believe in him whom he has sent" (6:29).

Several summers ago we were on our way from Wisconsin to Montana. Our youngest daughter, who was then eight, read somewhere about the Mt. Rushmore National Monument. She wanted to see it. I looked at the map and discovered that it was on the way and we could travel mostly interstates. So after spending a night with Dorothy's brother in Sparta, Wisconsin, we crossed Minnesota, and headed west on I-90 out of Sioux Falls, South Dakota. Along the way we read hundreds of signs about Walls Drug Store. We couldn't resist stopping and were pleasantly surprised. It was in fact a tourist trap, but not the stereotyped sort. The prices for food were surprisingly reasonable. After a refreshing tour of the drugstore we took off west toward Rapid City. We came upon an exit sign for route 16 and a sign "Mt. Rushmore National Monument." We saw the sign, but the mountain was nowhere in sight. In fact, from the exit it was twenty miles south into the Black Hills. The sign was important. It directed us to the reality. But it was not itself the reality. We never would have heard the last of it had we said to our daughter, "There's the sign. Now let's hurry on to Montana." In fact, the sign had no real meaning for her. So we turned down Highway 16, found a motel, and bright and early the next morning we stood in awe of the impressive likenesses of Washington, Jefferson, Lincoln, and Teddy Roosevelt, the four mugs on the mountain. She was now content. She experienced more than the sign. She gazed at length on the reality itself.

For John, the arrival at faith (that Jesus was sent from God) has its stages. The first stage is hearing the report of the sign (20:30,31). The second is a willingness to look beyond the sign to the reality at which it points (6:26). The third is the decision that Jesus is from beyond — he is the Holy One of God (6:69). Because of that faith one becomes God's when he is baptized by water and the Spirit (3:5).

The signs make possible the first step to faith. It is not, however, the reality. Many persons never take the time to see that toward which the sign points. That was true when Jesus lived; it is true now. There are those who hear of the mighty signs of Jesus, but they could care less and do not turn aside. Some notice the signs, turn off to see to what it is at which they point, but the fog of their presuppositions prevents them from a clear vision of what is behind the scenes. But a few see the sign, turn off to investigate, and pushing aside the mists, see Jesus for who he is, that is, the Son of God.

In John the works of Jesus lead to faith. The faith to which they lead is that Jesus is the Son of God; he is God (John 1:1). In the standard language of John he is one of a kind. The signs provide a basis for the inference as to who he is. He is the one sent from God.

## *Conclusion*

The work of Jesus is an inextricable aspect of his ministry. It declares that God is interested in more than what we believe or think. He sent his Son on a mission of doing good, of caring love. In that manner he defines being Godlike in the sphere of man. And he beckons us to take up the ways of his Son. May his love compel us to do likewise!

# Questions for Discussion

1. What do the mighty actions of Jesus mean?

2. How does Matthew see Jesus' message as related to his works?

3. Why did Jesus help the people who came to him?

4. Did Jesus do mighty works simply to prove his divinity?

5. In what way was the life of Jesus the way of the cross?

6. What is it that the disciples did not understand about Jesus' stilling the storm and feeding the multitudes?

7. Why did Luke think that people should pay attention when Jesus spoke?

8. Why did Luke show Jesus as having a special concern for women and the poor?

9. To what role did John assign the signs of Jesus in his Gospel?

10. Are there seven and only seven explicit signs of Jesus in the Gospel of John?

11. How do the signs lead to faith according to John?

12. Does preaching the Gospels include encouraging believers to help others?

# 6
# He Preached Good News

*J*esus was remembered as one who taught or preached. He proclaimed "the good news." He was a herald, the title given a periodic official newsbearer (*kerygma*, "proclamation"). As Peter reminded Cornelius,

> You know the message he sent to the people of Israel, preaching peace by Jesus Christ — he is Lord of all. That message spread throughout Judea, beginning in Galilee after the baptism . . . (Acts 10:36,37).

Jesus was identified as teacher (see, e. g., Matthew 8:19; 12:38; 19:16; 22:16; 22:24,36; 26:18) even more than as wonder worker.

Matthew stressed Jesus as a teacher, first, then as a healer.

> Jesus went throughout Galilee, teaching in their synagogues and proclaiming the good news of the kingdom and curing every disease and every sickness among the people. So his fame spread throughout all Syria (Matt. 4:23-24).

The teachers of Jesus' day were the scribes of the Pharisees. They taught young men interested in becoming

Rabbis like themselves to read the Torah, that is, the five books of Moses (the Pentateuch), and they taught synagogue attendees. Synagogues were scattered throughout the land of Palestine and in other countries wherever Jews lived. The Torah, the Prophets and the Writings were read aloud in the synagogues and then the scribes, or Rabbis, if present, discussed implications for contemporary life. Their teaching had authority because it was based upon the writings of Moses, the most revered of ancient teachers. Moses was a prophet. He received his teaching from God (Deut. 18:15-22).

At about the age thirty, Jesus began to speak in the synagogues around the Sea of Galilee where he grew up. He had great appeal as a teacher. He developed an impressive following. People returned again and again to hear what he had to say. The crowds became so enormous that a synagogue no longer was adequate. Matthew tells of an occasion in which Jesus climbed a mountainside so as to be able to address the massive audience (Matt. 5:1-2). More than one, no doubt, recalled that Moses had delivered the words of God to their forefathers while on a mountain. When Jesus ended his discourse the crowds were electrified. "Now when Jesus had finished saying these things, the crowds were astounded at his teaching, for he taught them as one having authority, and not as their scribes" (Matt. 7:28).

The scribes spent their time carefully explicating the law of Moses. Their authority was derived from his. In addition, they cited interpretations of specific texts by the greatest of the Rabbis. Jesus too commenced with the Scriptures and underlined their significance (Matt. 5:17-20). But when he explained the commandments, Jesus did not engage in lengthy eulogies of the ancient authors nor enumerate the interpretations of others. He set out his own perspectives as if he had achieved a new understanding. "You have heard that it was said to those of ancient times, 'You shall not murder'; and 'whoever murders shall be liable to judgment.' But I say to you that if you are angry with a brother or sister, you will be liable to judgment" (Matt. 5:21-22).

Some pondered whether Jesus was the prophet of whom Moses spoke. "The LORD your God will raise up for you a prophet like me from among your own people; you shall heed such a prophet" (Deut. 18:15). The priests thought perhaps John the Baptist presumed to be that prophet. "Are you the prophet?" But John replied, "No" (John 1:21). Later, as Jesus spoke in Jerusalem, some who heard were so impressed that they decided that he must be the one to whom Moses referred. "When they heard these words, some in the crowd said, 'This is really the prophet'" (John 7:40).

Jesus made an additional impact, because whenever he spoke, something happened! His credibility was phenomenal, since whatever he commanded came about. Mark particularly stressed how onlookers noticed results when Jesus spoke. "They were all amazed, and they kept on asking one another, 'What is this? A new teaching — with authority! He commands even the unclean spirits, and they obey him'" (1:27). It was not so much what Jesus said that was different. Jesus gained remarkable respect because whatever he said came about. Moses set out the criterion by which one may know whether a prophet is from God. "If a prophet speaks in the name of the LORD but the thing does not take place or prove true, it is a word that the LORD has not spoken" (Deut. 18:22). Jesus may indeed be the prophet, so the crowds concluded, because whatever he said took place.

Jimmy Carter was a dedicated, hard-working president. He came to Washington as an outsider. He surrounded himself with associates who had little or no connections with the Senate or House of Representatives. He cultivated the outsider image because he believed that the American people were fed up with professional politicians. They wanted fresh leadership without ties to the political past. Jimmy spent long hours researching the backgrounds of all the decisions he was called upon to make. But after a time, it became clear that the government was in gridlock. However appropriate Carter's directives and policies, he could not get Congress to act upon them. Because he had no ties to Congress, he could not marshal their backing. Carter proposed much excellent legislation for improving life in the United States and in the world. But little or nothing happened. Political observers soon questioned Carter's credibility. What good was an outsider president if his bills often ended up in the shredder? Jesus, in contrast, had incredible believability. Whenever he spoke something happened!

## *The Core of Jesus' Teaching*

Three affirmations of Jesus stand out: (1) the kingdom of God is imminent, (2) God is loving, merciful and just, and (3) humans should dedicate their lives to loving God and serving others. Jesus discussed many other topics, including the growth of the kingdom, the procedures of the church, the unity of those who believe, and the signs of the impending end of the age. Since later chapters take up the latter topics, additional comments on what Jesus taught on these subjects will be noted in the appropriate chapter.

### The Impending Kingdom

Jesus anticipated an impending end of life as the people of his times knew it. God, he declared, would break into human history in a new, unprecedented manner. "Repent, for the kingdom of heaven has come near" (Matt. 4:17). It was near because Jesus, Son of the king, was present.

> Once Jesus was asked by the Pharisees when the kingdom of God was coming, and he answered, "The kingdom of God is not coming with things that can be observed; nor will they say, 'Look, here it is!' or 'There it is!' For, in fact, the kingdom of God is among you" (Luke 17:20-21).

Jesus designed his teaching so that his hearers would know

what to do so as to get ready for the kingdom of God and enter it when the kingdom arrived.

Jesus not only announced the pending inbreaking of the kingdom. He set out, as he taught, what the kingdom of God is going to be like when it arrives, and what one must do who wishes to enter it. It is apparent that in Matthew's perception Jesus answered these questions in the sermon on the mount. After stating the above focus of Jesus' ministry Matthew reported the call of Peter, Andrew, James, and John to discipleship, and then declared: "Jesus went throughout Galilee, teaching in their synagogues and proclaiming the good news of the kingdom" (Matt. 4:23). Matthew followed immediately with the sermon on the mount.

The focus of the teaching of Jesus in the sermon on the mount and elsewhere is upon the love of God and the expected human response of, in turn, loving God and neighbor. Before taking up the sermon it is appropriate to notice key statements of Jesus which declare love as at the core of the kingly sway of God. One time a religious leader with expertise in the law of Moses (the Torah) was present as various detractors tried to best Jesus in argument. So this man put to Jesus the question which was often discussed among those who spent long hours with the Torah. "Teacher, which commandment in the law is the greatest?" The answer of Jesus puts love of God and neighbor at the heart of what the law is about, and for that matter the center of the teachings of Jesus (Matt. 22:37-40).

Jesus expressed a similar conviction as he commented upon the misplaced priorities of the scribes and Pharisees.

> Woe to you, scribes and Pharisees, hypocrites! For you tithe mint, dill, and cummin, and have neglected the weightier matters of the law: justice and mercy and faith. It is these you ought to have practiced without neglecting the others (Matt. 23:23).

Justice, mercy, and faith go a long way toward summing up the main foci of the "theology" of Jesus.

## The Sermon on the Mount
### Matthew 5:1–7:28

The sermon on the mount has fittingly been declared a fundamental expression of the commitment and deportment of those whom Jesus envisions as entering the impending kingdom of heaven. Toward the end of these teachings Jesus charged, "Not everyone who says to me, 'Lord, Lord,' will enter the kingdom of heaven, but only the one who does the will of my Father in Heaven" (Matt. 7:21). As the will of the Father was set out, Jesus declared, in his own instructions:

> **"All authority in heaven and on earth has been given to me. Go therefore and make disciples of all nations, baptizing them in the name of the Father and of the Son and of the Holy Spirit, and teaching them to obey everything that I have commanded you. And remember, I am with you always, to the end of the age" (Matt. 28:18-20).**

In the beatitudes Jesus stressed a humble attitude toward God which has profound old Testament roots. "Blessed are the poor in spirit, for theirs is the kingdom of heaven" (Matt. 5:3). The mourners, the meek, the merciful, and the peacemakers, all of which characterize those humbly dependent upon God, will likewise be blessed. All these look to God in awe and love. They hunger and thirst for righteousness, they are pure in heart, and they are willing even to undergo persecution. God and his kingdom are first in their lives. Such persons are salt and light (Matt. 5:13-15). In their actions they exhibit the caring actions of God. "Let your light shine before others, so that they may see your good works and give glory to your Father in heaven" (Matt. 5:16). They not only love God, they serve those around about them.

Those in the kingdom are dedicated to God's ways from of old. Jesus is the one who will bring the declarations of the law and the teachings of the prophets to fruition. "I have come not to abolish but to fulfill" (Matt. 5:17). The righteousness of those who take up the kingdom's ways will be greater than that of the scribes and Pharisees. One of the ways that righteousness will be exhibited is that the very heart itself will exhibit the love and purity of God. The attitude towards others should be love, not anger. The ways of the fathers put the emphasis on the overt act of murder. Jesus got to the root of the matter. If the heart is loving, murder will not occur (Matt. 5:21), and the conflicts with others will be resolved (Matt. 5:25). Adultery likewise commences in the heart (Matt. 5:28) and breaks up marriages (5:31). One should respect the rights of others and not set out to undermine them, and keep one's word. Compassion should flow for those who are needy (Matt. 5:38-42). Since God loves all humankind made in his image, those in his kingdom should do likewise (Matt. 5:44-48). The love for God and worship of him should be singular in motive and purity of heart.

The giving of alms should be for the love of God, not for show (Matt. 6:2). Prayer should be done in private since it is to God, not so as to impress one's associates. In the model prayer Jesus set out for the disciples, recognition is given to God as Father, and the disciples' dependence upon him for sustenance. The mercy God shows through forgiveness the disciple should extend to acquaintances (Matt. 6:12-14). Fasting should be done for its spiritual benefits, not in order to receive praise from the onlookers. Love should be focused upon God and people and not upon the treasures of earth (Matt. 6:19-24). God is faithful in supplying the needs of those who go with him, which frees up the disciples so that they may seek first his kingdom. "But strive first for the kingdom of God and his righteousness, and all these things will be given to you as well" (Matt. 6:33).

Since God is a God of mercy, disciples should be merciful, not judgmental toward others (Matt. 7:1). Guard the gifts God has supplied so that they may be employed for the good of humankind, and keep petitioning God since he knows human circumstances, and will supply what is needed

(Matt. 7:7-11). Disciples should consider the needs of others in the same manner that they themselves wish consideration (Matt. 7:12). On the road ahead we should seek that gate whereby we enter life. Many are vanquished because they enter the gate which leads to the course of least resistance. One has to watch out for false prophets and those who lead astray. The way to ascertain whether prophets are true or false is to size up their life and the outcome of their teachings. Whether a person is living by kingdom rules can be determined by their fruits (Matt. 7:19). Not all who call Jesus Lord will enter the kingdom, only those who hear the words of Jesus and act upon them (Matt. 7:24-27). The one who hears the words of Jesus and does them is building an indestructible life, just as the person who builds a house upon a rock. Those who follow the course of least resistance and ignore the lifestyle recommended by Jesus will face catastrophe, just like a house built upon the sand.

We lived for ten years in California. While we were there, we experienced two major earthquakes. We didn't know much about earthquakes before moving to California, but we learned fast. One of the things we learned was that houses built on solid rock usually come through earthquakes without damage, while those built on alluvial plains or fill, often ended up with cracks, roofs caved in and items strewn all over the house. We had the good fortune that our condo on the Pepperdine University, Malibu, was built on a solid rock bluff. While we felt the earthquakes as much as anyone else, we suffered no damage at all nor did we have any item fall to the floor from counters or shelves. A quarter of a mile away the School of Law library built on fill, regularly had books scattered on the floor following an earthquake.

Jesus declared that a life built upon God's characteristics of love, mercy, compassion, and singularity of heart will thrive and survive. That is the solid rock foundation that will lead to life. The impending kingdom is on the way. A turnaround is required. The signs of the kingdom of God were present right in their very midst in the mighty works of Jesus. "But if it is by the Spirit of God that I cast out demons, then the kingdom of God has come to you" (Matt. 12:28).

Those who enter the kingdom will love God and humankind, but they will likewise exhibit faith that Jesus can do the work of God. A centurion whose servant was ill requested that Jesus cure him. Jesus proposed to go where the servant lay, but the centurion told him that he was accustomed to giving orders and having them carried out. He believed that if Jesus gave the order for his servant's cure, it would happen! Jesus gave the order and the servant was healed that very hour (Matt. 8:13).

In regard to the centurion's faith, Jesus expressed amazement: "When Jesus heard him, he was amazed and said to those who followed him, 'Truly I tell you, in no one in Israel have I found such faith'" (Matt. 8:11-12).

The kingdom of God is manifest in the ministry of Jesus. Those who expect to eat at table with God's great servants of the past must believe that Jesus is of God, love his Father, and enter into a loving relationship with those who occupy their space.

### Being Rich toward God

In the Gospel of Luke is a section of Jesus' comments and arresting parables (Luke 10–19), several of which are not found in the other Gospels. A thread running through these various sayings is that possessions are God given and are to be employed in assisting others. As Jesus stated earlier,

> Give, and it will be given to you. A good measure, pressed down, shaken together, running over, will be put into your lap; for the measure you give will be the measure you get back (Luke 6:38).

One time an expert in the Torah set out to test Jesus. "Teacher," he said, "what must I do to inherit eternal life?"

(Luke 10:25). Jesus put the question back to him. "What is written in the law?" The lawyer responded, "You shall love the Lord your God with all your heart, and with all your soul, and with all your strength, and with all your mind; and your neighbor as yourself" (Luke 10:28). Jesus commended his reply. The question is then who the neighbor is that one is to love. Can a definition be given of "neighbor" which limits liability? If not, the demand seems endless. Jesus set out no general guidelines, but told a story about a man who was beaten up and left to die by robbers as he went from Jerusalem to Jericho. This parable has come to be identified by the nationality of the person who helped him, thus the Good Samaritan.

As the injured man lay there, religious leaders walked by and made no effort to help him, including a priest and a Levite. Finally a Samaritan came along. A good Jew typically did not even speak to a Samaritan, so inferior was one of that nationality perceived to be. The Samaritan had pity when he saw the man and bandaged his wounds, after having poured oil and wine on them. He loaded him on his pack animal and left him at an inn. He left money for his care, and told the innkeeper that when he returned he would pay for any additional required. Jesus ended with a question. "Which of these three, do you think, was a neighbor to the man who fell into the hands of the robbers?" The lawyer responded, "The one who showed him mercy" (Luke 10:37). To love one's neighbor demands not so much the alleviation of the all the world's needs, but of those with whom one comes in contact who need help, whether they are of one's own clan and liking or not. God has given so that we may give.

On another occasion as Jesus spoke of mistreatment, someone in the crowd asked him to command his brother to divide the family inheritance according to the rules. Jesus refused to be an arbitrator, but warned against greed. He then told a parable about a man whose land was productive to superfluity. This man of newly-gained wealth decided that in order to store the abundance he would tear down his barns and build bigger ones. He would thereby be secure and could relax, eat, drink, and be merry. But God called him a fool and informed him that his life would be demanded that very night. Jesus ended by saying, "So it is with those who store up treasures for themselves but are not rich toward God" (Luke 12:21).

What does it mean to be rich toward God? To be rich toward God is to trust him for basic needs (Luke 12:22-31). It is to employ the treasures provided by God for others.

> Do not be afraid, little flock, for it is your Father's good pleasure to give you the kingdom. Sell your possessions, and give alms. Make purses for yourselves that do not wear out, an unfailing treasure in heaven, where no thief comes near and no moth destroys. For where your treasure is, there your heart will be also (Luke 12:32-34).

The point is emphasized further in that after charging his hearers to be dressed and ready for the arrival of the groom at the wedding banquet, Peter asked who this parable was for (Luke 12:41). Jesus implied by his answer that it was for everyone. But he also made clear that to be ready at the master's return is to utilize what God has given so as to supply the needs of others. "And the Lord said, 'Who then is the faithful and prudent manager whom his master will put in charge of his slaves, to give them their allowance of food at the proper time?'" (Luke 12:42). When the disciples who are rich toward God give a banquet they do not invite the rich and famous. They should invite those who actually need a good meal (Luke 14:12-14).

Jesus followed these instructions with the parable of the great dinner or banquet. A servant was sent to invite friends and acquaintances of the host. But those invited all alike had "valid" excuses for not coming (Luke 14:21-23).

Luke's interest in highlighting the need of the disciples to use their possessions to benefit others is clear in comparing this parable with another one about a great banquet in Matthew. In Matthew the ones invited after the first group has declined were "everyone" implying that the Jews rejected the invitation of Jesus and therefore all the nations would be invited in their stead (Matt. 22:1-10).

What about people who have spent a fortune on themselves rather than on others? Jesus told about just such a person, in the story commonly identified as the parable of the Prodigal Son. "A few days later the younger son gathered all he had and traveled to a distant country, and there he squandered his property in dissolute living" (Luke 15:13). Such a person is received by the Father with open arms if they return. They may not recover the inheritance they squandered since the older brother still gets what is rightfully his (Luke 15:31), but they live once again in the father's house, and are nurtured and sustained by him (Luke 15:32).

The parable of the shrewd manager has been a puzzle to many, but it seems to make sense if seen in light of the trajectory that God gives in order that people in turn will give to others. The rich man in the parable is obviously God. The manager is any person to whom God has supplied an abundance. Such a person has been assigned by God to manage the gifts as God intended (Luke 16:1). When the manager was taken to task for "squandering" the property, he then starting helping others. To one he reduced by half what was owed the master, to another a fifth. In effect, therefore, he shared the master's resources rather that expending them on himself as did the prodigal son. What the man did was dishonest by the rules, then and now, but not by God's rules. He wants those who are his to reduce the fiduciary demands on others by freely giving away his gifts. He still lays claims upon the resources under our control. We think they are ours, but we manage them for him. The shrewd manager did what he did as a "worldling" as we might say, so as to feather his own nest. By his actions he presumed the people he had helped would in turn help him when he lost his management position. "You scratch my back, and I will scratch yours." "The children of this world are more shrewd in dealing with their own generation than are the children of light" (Luke 16:8). If the children of light were as shrewd as these "worldlings," they would recognize that God will welcome into his presence those who have shared with others the possessions with which he has supplied them. "I tell you, make friends for yourselves by means of dishonest wealth so that when it is gone, they may welcome you into the eternal homes" (Luke 16:9). The picture here is that those we have helped who have gone on before will be present at the time of our entry into the place of God and will speak a word on our behalf so that we may we enter.

Grant Newton was a Professor of Business Administration at Pepperdine University. But he was even more noted as a consultant to companies restructuring after bankruptcy. In the early 1980s Grant and his wife Valda finally gave in to the implorings of Bill Stivers, Professor of Spanish and other romance languages. Bill had, for some years, started, looked after, and raised money for several churches and programs in Mexico south of San Diego. These consisted of mission points and a medical clinic in Tijuana, a children's home in Ensenada, and a church, a youth camp and a house building project in San Felipe. Upon visiting these works the Newtons caught the vision. They had been blessed by God, and they soon commenced employing their considerable resources to help those far less fortunate in Mexico. They especially focused on San Felipe. They helped build and repair structures at the youth camp and recruited Pepperdine students to work there in the summers. Twice a year they arranged to build a house in the city. Members of the church in San Felipe had equipment for making adobe blocks. The Newtons arranged to take the rest of the materials down from California. They recruited persons from the Pepperdine student body and the Malibu Church to assist them. God gave to them. They in turn used his magnificence to help others.

The basis of wealth for believer and unbeliever alike is God. Maine is famous for its forests, lobsters, and potatoes. Those who obtain wealth through the sale of these products never created a single tree, lobster, or potato. Texas is famous for oil, cattle, and chemicals. But no Texan ever created a drop of crude, a cow, or the minerals from which to synthesize chemicals. California is famous for oranges, almonds, and real estate developments. Many a person has become wealthy from each. But no Californian ever created an orange, an almond, or an inch of a tract of ground. All of us manage that to which we have no clear title, even though we may possess such a government-generated document. God ultimately holds a title to everything. "For every wild animal of the forest is mine, the cattle on a thousand hills" (Ps. 50:10).

The same point is made in the parable of the rich man and Lazarus. The rich man wouldn't lift a finger to help Lazarus who lay at his gate covered with sores. When Lazarus died, however, God graciously addressed all his needs (Luke 16:19-22). He was comforted in the bosom of Abraham. Later the rich man died and in Hades he was tormented day and night. He looked across a great chasm and saw that Lazarus was profusely blessed. The rich man begged Abraham for mercy, and implored him that he send Lazarus to "dip the tip of his finger in water and cool my tongue; for I am in agony in these flames" (Luke 16:24). But Abraham refused. Lazarus could give no favorable testimony on behalf of the rich man. The rich man refused to lift his finger in this life to help Lazarus, so Abraham in the life beyond refused to permit Lazarus to lift a finger to help the rich man!

This trajectory ends with the contrast of two wealthy men. The first was a ruler who came to Jesus and asked, "Good Teacher, what must I do to inherit eternal life?" (Luke 18:18). Jesus first referred him to the ten commandments, whereupon the ruler insisted that he had kept all of them from his youth. Jesus then instructed him, "Sell all that you own and distribute the money to the poor, and you will have treasure in heaven [the way to be rich toward God]; then come, follow me" (Luke 18:22). This command of Jesus made him sad for he was very rich. He could not find it in his heart to do what Jesus said to do.

The second man responded differently. He was a wealthy tax collector named Zacchaeus. Zacchaeus had heard of Jesus and wanted to see him so badly that he climbed a tree. Jesus invited him down and himself to his house. Jesus so impressed Zacchaeus that he blurted out, "Look, half of my possessions, Lord, I will give to the poor; and if I have defrauded anyone of anything, I will pay back four times as much" (Luke 19:8). Zacchaeus was on the way. He redirected the affluence provided by God. Upon coming face to face with Jesus he set out to share what he had accumulated with others. And Jesus praised his decision. "Today salvation has come to this house, because he too is a son of Abraham" (v. 9). Jesus did not condemn persons of wealth because they were wealthy. He condemned them only when they squandered their wealth on themselves rather than sharing it with others.

The message of Jesus is powerful and heart quickening. He set out to remake God's world over into a place where love is pervasive and where people are attuned to his changing this world and preparing it for an imminent end.

# Questions for Discussion

1. What is the importance of teaching in Jesus' ministry?

2. Why were Jesus' listeners impressed with his authority?

3. What was the ultimate source of Jesus' authority?

4. What were core teachings of Jesus?

5. Jesus believed that the kingdom was already existent in the present. On what grounds?

6. What are some of the kingdom guidelines in the Sermon on the Mount?

7. How do God's love and human love provide the key for unlocking Jesus' teaching?

8. What should one do if one has more than enough according to Jesus?

9. How can one become rich toward God?

10. In what way was the shrewd manager wiser than the children of light?

11. Why wouldn't Abraham permit Lazarus to put water on the rich man's tongue?

12. Did Jesus condemn Zacchaeus because he only gave half of what he had?

# 7
# He Gave His Life a Ransom for Many

As Peter put it in his sermon, "They put him to death by hanging him on a tree; but God raised him on the third day and allowed him to appear, not to all the people but to us who were chosen by God as witnesses, and who ate and drank with him after he rose from the dead" (Acts 10:39-41).

The cross is the focal point for the Christ of the New Testament and therefore for the New Testament itself. This is true not only of the Gospels but of most of the Epistles. Paul wrote to the Corinthians, singling out what, for him, is of most importance.

> For I handed on to you as of first importance what I in turn had received: that Christ died for our sins in accordance with the scriptures, and that he was buried, and that he was raised on the third day in accordance with the scriptures, and that he appeared to Cephas, then to the twelve (1 Cor. 15:3-5).

Earlier in the letter Paul wrote: "For I decided to know nothing among you except Jesus Christ, and him crucified" (1 Cor. 2:2).

## *They Will Kill Him*

Early in all the Gospels it is clear that the history-transforming life of Jesus of Nazareth culminated in his crucifixion. The Gospels set out the details of Jesus' death and the empty tomb that followed. But little reflecting or theologizing on what he accomplished by his death is found in them. That is fleshed out in the Epistles, especially those of Paul. The Gospel writers, with John being something of an exception, focused on the details of Jesus' life and death.

Once Zechariah the father of John the Baptist recovered his voice, he uttered an oracle as to the significance of John. John's importance lay in his role in preparing the way of the Lord. "For you will go before the Lord to prepare his ways, to give knowledge of salvation to his people by the forgiveness of their sins" (Luke 1:76-77). Just how Jesus would forgive sins was not clear, but the means will be disclosed before the Gospel story is complete. Clearly Jesus is Savior and Messiah, the Lord (Luke 2:11). Simeon, the prophet, foretold that Jesus would become a light to all humankind; to the Gentiles as well as to the Jews (Luke 2:32). Jesus commenced his public proclamation in Capernaum and almost immediately alienated certain religious leaders. They drove him out of town and hoped to kill him (Luke 4:24).

In the Gospel of Mark, perhaps more than elsewhere, not only is Jesus' death *upon* the cross, but his life itself is the way of the cross. It is not until the Gospel is half through that the disciples openly express their conclusion that this one they followed and with whom they ate meals was indeed the Messiah (Mark 8:30). It took them a long time to put two and two together. One would think that the day upon which Peter blurted out, "You are the Messiah," would have been a climactic moment in Jesus' life. That which Jesus had long sought finally occurred! But Jesus almost immediately put aside the euphoria. It is not enough to confess that Jesus is

Messiah. It is more important to recognize the nature of his messianic role. The way of the Messiah is not the glory road. It was not the occupying of marble and cedar palaces. It was not the employment of multiple servants for beck and call day and night. It was not a constant review of foot soldiers, horsemen and chariots. Jesus was a suffering servant. His life was the way of the cross, and he was consigned for death on the cross. "Then he began to teach them that the Son of Man must undergo great suffering, and be rejected by the elders, the chief priests, and the scribes, and be killed, and after three days risen again" (Mark 8:31). Peter was still contemplating the glory that would be theirs as followers of the anointed king. As he heard Jesus speak, he became deeply disturbed. He took Jesus aside and began to rebuke him. Jesus in turn rebuked Peter, "Get behind me, Satan! For you are setting your mind not on divine things but on human things" (Mark 8:33).

At that point Jesus disabused those who thought his Messianic rule would bring fame and fortune to those who followed him. Just as the life of the Messiah was one of servanthood, so also is the life of the disciple.

In 1989 we went to Alaska with our oldest daughter and family. We traveled by car ferry across Prince William Sound about two months after the Valdez oil spill. From Valdez we drove to Denali National Park which is larger than the state of Massachusetts. Going interior almost two hundred miles, we stayed four days in a private camp. It was a beautiful setting. From the front door of our cabin we were able to see rising high above the terrain majestic Mount McKinley. On the second morning one option was to climb the elevation behind the camp. Dorothy has never been much into mountain climbing so with much encouragement from all of us, and telling her that by looking she could see that it wasn't that much of a climb, we persuaded her to go along. The first part of the trail was through tundra which made the going difficult since we sank into the muck above the ankles. After about an hour on the trail with a few stops to regain breath, we finally arrived at the height we could see from the camp. But we, and especially Dorothy, were in for a rude awakening. That was not in fact the top. Ahead was another peak. The peak we could see from camp was not the real peak. It was a false peak. Dorothy was ready to go back down, but we finally convinced her to go on because no one else wanted to return to camp.

The disciples of Jesus reached a peak when they confessed that Jesus was the Messiah. But Jesus was aware the sort of Messiah they hoped for was not the one he came to be. There was still another peak for them to climb. Some of the disciples at least believed that by allying themselves with Jesus they would share in fame and acclaim. "Grant us to sit, one at your right hand and one at your left, in your glory" (Mark 10:37). They reached a peak. They recognized that God was doing great things through Jesus. They wanted a part. But they misunderstood. They thought about power from a human perspective.

> You know that among the Gentiles those whom they recognize as their rulers lord it over them. But it is not so among you; but whoever wishes to become great among you must be your servant, and whoever wishes to be first among you must be slave of all. For the Son of Man came not to be served but to serve, and to give his life a ransom for many (Mark 10:42-45).

It is clear from this statement that the life Jesus modeled for the disciples was the way of the cross. He showed them by his life what it was to abandon the glory road for the servant road.

> He called the crowd with his disciples, and said to them, "If any want to become my followers, let them deny themselves and take up their cross and follow me. For those who want to save their life will lose it, and those who lose their life for my sake, and for the sake of the gospel, will save it" (Mark 8:34-35).

## *And to Give His Life a Ransom for Many*

For the first time in the statement "Give his life a ransom for many" (also Matt. 20:28) Jesus gave a hint as to what he was to accomplish by his death. His death would not be just any death. It would be a death in which many would be ransomed. We may presume release from sin, Satan, and death. The imagery is from the arena of human slavery which was rampant in the ancient world. In the epistles this metaphor is explored even more. So in the synoptics, that is, Matthew, Mark, and Luke, we learn that Jesus planned to give his life for the release of many in bondage.

Another way in which Jesus made the same point was by his remarks at the last supper, "[F]or this is my blood of the covenant, which is poured out for many for the forgiveness of sins" (Matt. 26:26-28). The image is from the sacrifice which was likewise pervasive in the ancient world. Jesus announced that his death was sacrificial, that is, that by his broken body and spilt blood the sins of many would be forgiven. In Mark the declaration is "This is my blood of the covenant, which is poured out for many" (Mark 14:24, see also Luke 22:20). The tie with the remission of sins is again declared in Luke 24: "and that repentance and forgiveness of sins is to be proclaimed in his name to all nations, beginning from Jerusalem" (Luke 24:47).

## *Behold the Lamb of God*

The Gospel of John supplies more theological insights on the death and resurrection from the first than do the Synoptics. One day while John the Baptist was talking with two of his disciples, Jesus appeared in the distance. John turned and said to them, "Here is the Lamb of God who takes away the sin of the world!" (John 1:29). The imagery is sacrificial (Lev. 14:10-13). Jesus removed the sin stains from those who are at enmity with God. Jesus spoke of his death early in his ministry according to John. On the first Passover after he commenced his ministry, Jesus went to Jerusalem, and upon overturning the tables of the money changers, the Pharisees asked him for a sign. Jesus responded, "Destroy this temple, and in three days I will raise it up" (John 2:19). The famous statement in John 3:16 claimed even more for the death of Jesus than forgiveness of sins. Through Jesus those who believe "may not perish but may have eternal life." Jesus affirmed the same grand boon for humankind later as he discussed his body as the bread of life. "Those who eat my flesh and drink my blood have eternal life, and I will raise them up on the last day; for my flesh is true food and my blood is true drink" (John 6:54-55). The death of Jesus, according to John, was the ground for the forgiveness of human sin; the resurrection was the avenue through which Jesus gave everlasting life. "I am the living bread that came down from heaven. Whoever eats of this bread will live forever; and the bread that I will give for the life of the world is my flesh" (John 6:51).

In the Gospel of John statements and events often have two meanings, one for the person making it, and a different one for those who later witnessed the death and resurrection of Christ. The Pharisees learned of the resurrection of Lazarus, and they were disturbed to no end. They were fearful that Jesus' fame as a miracle worker would sweep the country like wildfire through California chapparral. The chief priests and Pharisees called a meeting. One expressed fear that if Jesus continued to create disturbances, the Romans would destroy the temple and the nation. The high priest Caiaphas argued that the only solution was to assassinate Jesus so as to avoid religious upheaval. "You do not understand that it is better for you to have one man die for the people than to have the whole nation destroyed" (John 11:50). Caiaphas was right in a way he did not comprehend. Perhaps decimation by the Romans could thereby be avoided. But that was not the real purpose of Jesus' death. It was in fact for the nation in a more strategic sense.

> He did not say this on his own, but being high priest that year he prophesied that Jesus was about to die for the nation, and not for the nation only, but to gather into one the dispersed children of God. So from that day on they planned to put him to death (John 11:51-53).

The death of Jesus was in fact for the nation Israel. But it was also for all peoples, that is, all the dispersed children of God. The life of Jesus, as well as his death, was on behalf of others.

The death of Jesus was a real event in the life of God. "The Word was with God, and the Word was God" (John 1:1). In that sense it was objective. The atonement Jesus achieved was objective in that something happened in the very life of God himself.

The death of Jesus likewise, however, elicits a death in the disciple. Just as Jesus served in life and death, the disciple is to take up a lifestyle of service. In the Synoptics it was expressed in the charge, "If any want to become my followers, let them deny themselves and take up their cross and follow me" (Mark 8:34). In the Gospel of John the same point is made when Jesus washed the disciples feet. So just as the cross has an objective significance because it is a real event in the life of God, it also has a subjective (that is, in the subject, or humankind) significance in that it is replicated as a real experience in the life of the disciple.

Jesus came with his disciples to the Passover meal. During the meal he got up, took off his outer robe, tied a towel around his waist, and poured water into a basin. He went around the circle and washed the disciples feet, then dried them with the towel. What was surprising was not that feet were washed. It was conventional for household servants to wash the feet of dinner guests. What was unusual was who it was who washed feet. Jesus who "had come from God and was going to God" washed feet (John 13:3). Amazing! Peter was the one who broke the silence. "Lord, are you going to wash my feet?" (John 13:6). Peter adamantly declared, "You will never wash my feet" (John 13:8). Jesus assured Peter that he would understand later,

Peter thought like many of us. If the Lord is going to come into our presence, we have to get our act together and clean up our surroundings. We need to be spotless as the Savior enters. I heard a sermon once which raised the question, "What would you do if Jesus visited your house today?" The observation in the sermon was that you would vacuum the whole house. You would dust all the furniture. You would get out the best linens and towels. You would seek to sparkle for the master! But when Jesus visits, he does not seek the cleanest part of the house or our person. He goes for what is smelly, seamy and soiled. He approaches us at the feet. There is no way in which we can clean up aspects of our life. We have done things we are too ashamed to mention to those closest to us. But it is there Jesus meets us. And he washes our feet.

So Jesus said to Peter, "Unless I wash you, you have no share with me" (John 13:8). And neither will we. Because of his death, we enter the waters of baptism. We are washed. We arise clean. Peter was convinced. "Lord, not my feet only but also my hands and my head!" (John 13:9).

Why did Jesus die? He died to make us clean. The one who came from God and returned to God, washed us. At that moment we were pure as newly driven snow. By this very act he freed us to wash the feet of others even though they are smelly and seamy. Because we have been washed, we can now wash in turn. "So if I, your Lord and Teacher, have washed your feet, you also ought to wash one another's feet. For I have set you an example, that you also should do as I have done to you" (John 13:14-15). By an act of Jesus who was with God and who is God we are made clean. The cross was an objective event in the life of God. But now in turn, it is to become an event in the life of the believer. The atonement as set forth in Scripture is objective in God and subjective in the believer.

## God Was in Christ Reconciling the World to Himself

We have already noticed the centrality Paul gave to the cross in the gospel and in his preaching (1 Cor. 15:1-4). Paul declared that the death of Christ was a real moment in the very being of God. "In Christ God was reconciling the world to himself, not counting their trespasses against them, and entrusting the message of reconciliation to us" (2 Cor. 5:19). The main affirmation of Paul in regard to the death of Christ was that it was for the sins of humankind. It is not clear just what Scriptures Paul advanced so as to establish the efficacy of Christ's death. It may be from the wider claims of Scriptures brought together in such a manner as in Romans 5 drawing upon Genesis, especially chapters 2 and 3, and Jeremiah 31. In 1 Corinthians 5:7 he employed the comparison of the sacrificed lamb: "For our paschal lamb, Christ, has been sacrificed." Also in Romans, he wrote: "Through the redemption that is in Christ Jesus, whom God put forward as a sacrifice of atonement by his blood, effective through faith" (Rom. 3:24-25, compare Lev. 23:26-36). Paul also argued that Christ in his crucifixion attained victory over death, so that by the cross humans receive the privilege of life everlasting. "So that, just as sin exercised dominion in death, so grace might also exercise dominion through justification leading to eternal life through Jesus Christ our Lord" (Rom. 5:21).

In Romans 5, Paul developed in some detail his conviction that justification, that is, acceptance by God, came about as the result of Christ's death. The root metaphors have to do with estrangement and reconciliation in personal relationship. Christ died to reconcile those, who by violating and flouting God's expectations, were estranged from him.

> For if while we were enemies, we were reconciled to God through the death of his Son, much more surely, having been reconciled, will we be saved by his life (Rom. 5:10).

Paul developed his argument based on Adam as the door through which sin entered the world. Since the progenitor for humankind opened the door for estrangement, so in a new man, who was the very Son of God, the means of reconciliation was procured. The argument was therefore developed from Scripture even though the conclusion was not immediately apparent in Scripture. "For if the many died through the one man's trespass, much more surely have the grace of God and the free gift in the grace of the one man, Jesus Christ, abounded for many" (Rom. 5:15).

In Ephesians and Colossians the ramifications of the death of Christ take on cosmic proportions. The import of the cross, of course, was for humans. "And you who were once estranged and hostile in mind, doing evil deeds, he has now reconciled in his fleshly body through death (Col. 1:21). But the cross as an event in human time and space, reached beyond into all existence. "For in him all the fullness of God was pleased to dwell, and through him God was pleased to reconcile to himself all things, whether on earth or in heaven, by making peace through the blood of his cross" (Col. 1:19-20). In Ephesians the claim is that God, in devising the event upon earth, also incorporated ramifications for it for all that is: "according to his good pleasure that he set forth in Christ, as a plan for the fullness of time, to gather up all things in him, things in heaven and things on earth" (Eph. 1:9-10). Because of his death and by his resurrection Jesus became the Lord of all in the universe for this age and the age to come (Eph. 1:20-23). So the cross as an event in the life of God had ramifications far beyond its earthly manifestation.

## *Our Old Self Was Crucified with Him*

Even though Paul presented the case for the cross as an objective act of God in behalf of humankind and the cosmos, he spent much more time discussing the implications of the cross for human self-understanding and action. In Romans the first implication of the cross is that boasting is excluded. Justification does not come about through keeping the Torah but by faith in the Christ event (Rom. 3:27-31). Because of the cross, believers humbly receive the amazing grace God has bestowed, and now they boast of what God has done, rather than of any accomplishments of their own (Rom. 5:11). Second, because of the cross believers are to put sin out of their lives. "Therefore we have been buried with him by baptism into death, so that, just as Christ was raised from the dead by the glory of the Father, so we too might walk in newness of life" (Rom. 6:4). Furthermore, "Our old self was crucified with him so that the body of sin might be destroyed, and we might no longer be enslaved to sin" (Rom. 6:6). Third, because of the cross the allure of law keeping is terminated. "You have died to the law through the body of Christ" (Rom. 7:4). But not only are believers free from the allure of law, they are, fourth, released from the power and fear of death (Rom. 8:2,32).

> For I am convinced that neither death, nor life, nor angels, nor rulers, nor things present, nor things to come, nor powers, nor height, nor depth, nor anything else in all creation, will be able to separate us from the love of God in Christ Jesus our Lord (Rom. 8:38-39).

Fifth, because of Christ's death and one's status as the result, believers should assign similar worth to fellow believers. "For by the grace given to me I say to everyone among you not to think of yourself more highly than you ought to think" (Rom. 12:3; see also Phil. 2:3-11). In regard to matters over which personal backgrounds are diverse, being considerate, in view of the cross is important. "Do not let what you eat cause the ruin of one for whom Christ died" (Rom. 14:15; also 1 Cor. 8:11). Rather, "Welcome one another, therefore, just as Christ has welcomed you, for the glory of God" (Rom. 15:7). Ethnic preferences are to be respected.

In 1 Corinthians Paul advanced additional ways in which the cross becomes the grounds for life style. Preferences for different church leaders should disappear because it is only Christ who died for the believers. "Was Paul crucified for you?" (1 Cor. 1:13). "So let no one boast about human leaders" (1 Cor. 3:21). Second, the cross exhibits the wisdom of God which is the true reality transcending all other claims to wisdom (1 Cor. 1:21). Third, the life of the one who goes with Christ is like his, the way of the cross (1 Cor. 4:11-13).

Paul wrote much more about the style of the true apostle and minister being the way of the cross in 2 Corinthians. "Therefore I am content with weaknesses, insults, hardships, persecutions, and calamities for the sake of Christ; for whenever I am weak, then I am strong" (2 Cor. 12:10). Fourth, the cross frees one from exercising one's own rights so that God may be glorified. "Nevertheless, we have not made use of this right, but we endure anything rather than put an obstacle in the way of the gospel of Christ" (1 Cor. 9:12). The right of which Paul spoke was accepting money for his work with the church. Fifth, the cross means that whenever the Lord's supper is observed, believers should wait for one another, taking on the role of a servant (1 Cor. 11:17-34).

Paul especially commended the cross-style life in Galatians. Here, as in Romans, he asserted that the Christian is dead to the law because of Christ's crucifixion (Gal. 2:19-20; 5:3-6). The cross also becomes the grounds for eradicating the works of the flesh. "And those who belong to Christ Jesus have crucified the flesh with its passions and desires" (Gal. 5:24). But it is especially in regard to items reflecting ethnicity that Paul argued that the cross helped believers move beyond these barriers. The truth of the gospel (Gal.

2:5,14) was that salvation is by faith in Christ, not by any exterior mark whether it be circumcision, skin color, and religious or social conventions. "And we have come to believe in Christ Jesus, so that we might be justified by faith in Christ, and not by doing the works of the law, because no one will be justified by the works of the law" (Gal. 2:16). Because of the death of Jesus Christ, "There is no longer Jew or Greek, there is no longer slave or free, there is no longer male and female; for all of you are one in Christ Jesus" (Gal. 3:28). The cross has ultimate and irrevocable bearing on life in so many different ways.

In Ephesians the cross forms the ground rules for husband and wife, parent and children, and employer and employee relationships. The key text is Ephesians 5:1-2: "Therefore be imitators of God, as beloved children, and live in love, as Christ loved us and gave himself up for us, a fragrant offering and sacrifice to God." Christ gave himself up for us. He did this by his life and in his death. He therefore put aside his own prerogatives to fulfill human needs. He subjected himself to humanity. From the prior submission of Christ, Paul identified the ground which informs all human relationships. "Be subject to one another out of reverence for Christ" (Eph. 5:21). To be subject to one another shows reverence for Christ because he established the model. He himself was subject. Believers in turn are to be subject to Christ.

First Paul applied the model to the husband/wife relationship. "Wives, be subject to your husbands as you are to the Lord" (Eph. 5:22). The husbands in turn are to "love your wives, just as Christ loved the church and gave himself up for her" (Eph. 5:25). Some think a distinction is to be made between being subject and loving, but it is Christ, who by his death set the pattern for both so that love and being subject refer to the same phenomenon. Second, he applied it to the child/parent relationship. Children are to obey their parents "in the Lord" (Eph. 6:1). "In the Lord" likely has the same bearing as "in reverence for Christ." Fathers, in turn, are to have the welfare of their children at heart: "do not provoke your children to anger" (Eph. 6:4). In that sense they are sub-ject to their children. Finally, slaves are to obey their earthly masters in the same manner in which they obey Christ (Eph. 6:5). Their service is to be rendered as to the Lord, recalling his own subjection and servanthood (Eph. 6:7). Masters are to act in kind, "do the same to them," that is, look out for their interests. No favoritism is to be shown, for God himself is impartial (Eph. 6:9). The lives of all in their relationships are therefore to be informed by the cross.

## *To Remove Sin by the Sacrifice of Himself*

For the Hebrews writer Christ was important for what he accomplished. He created the worlds, "he . . . made purifi-cation for sins," then he sat down on the right hand of the majesty on high so as to be priest forever (Heb. 1:2-4). He was both sacrifice and sacrificer. His work takes on a para-mount significance because he "is the reflection of God's glory and the exact imprint of God's very being" (Heb. 1:3). Whatever God is, that also is the Son. He preexisted his entry on earth since "for a little while [he] was made lower than the angels" (Heb. 2:9). But following his death and his ascendancy he was once again with God.

Jesus not only bore the form of God, he took on a human form. He did this so that his death was on behalf of humans. "He had to become like his brothers and sisters in every respect, so that he might be a merciful and faithful high priest in the service of God" (Heb. 2:17). "For we do not have a high priest who is unable to sympathize with our weak-nesses, but we have one who in every respect has been tested as we are, yet without sin" (Heb. 4:15). Jesus, as the very image of God, was born as a babe. He grew up coping with childhood diseases. He was at the mercy of his parents. He sometimes was taunted and ridiculed by his youthful acquaintances. He survived adolescence with its awkwardness and uncertainty. He entered manhood. He knew the heat of the noonday sun. He perspired from manual labor. He fanned aside the dust from the road. He was truly God, truly man.

Jesus is the perfect priest. He is also the perfect sacrifice. He is the perfect sacrifice first because he entered, not the earthly tabernacle with his own blood, but the heavenly tabernacle.

> [H]e entered once for all into the Holy Place, not with the blood of goats and calves, but with his own blood, thus obtaining eternal redemption (Heb. 9:12; see also v. 24).

Not only was the heavenly tabernacle forever, since he himself was forever, so also was his blood which he offered up for humankind. It was far superior to the blood of bulls and goats since their blood is finite and remits only those sins for which it is offered. But the eternal blood of Christ was offered once for all.

> [S]o Christ, having been offered once to bear the sins of many, will appear a second time, not to deal with sin, but to save those who are eagerly waiting for him (Heb. 9:28).

The Hebrews writer was clear that the blood of bulls and goats removed sin.

> For if the blood of goats and bulls, with the sprinkling of the ashes of a heifer, sanctifies those who have been defiled so that their flesh is purified (Heb. 9:13).

But their blood could not remove sin forever. Christ's blood removed sin once for all.

If a Jew unwittingly ate pork, he took a sacrifice to the temple so as to obtain forgiveness. If two years later the same violation reoccurred, a new sacrifice was required. It wasn't that the blood of bulls and goats did not take away sin (Heb. 10:4); it did not take sin away forever. The blood of Christ in one act of sacrifice, however, removes all sins, present and future. "For by a single offering he has perfected for all time those who are sanctified" (Heb. 10:14).

By his one-time sacrifice, Jesus removed even the memory or consciousness of sin. After having offered an animal sacrifice for sin, the sacrificer remains painfully aware of being a sinner, since a new sin demands a new sacrifice, "gifts and sacrifices are offered that cannot perfect the conscience of the worshiper" (Heb. 9:9). Before Christ's once for all sacrifice humans could only constantly visualize themselves as sinners. But with the once for all sacrifice of Christ, though the believer is aware that sin is likely to happen in the future, the weight of sin does not burden the conscience because Christ in his death has already paid it all. It is like word processing. When there were only manual typewriters, persons like me always bore the self-image of being a poor typist. But when I commenced using word processing, it was no longer necessary to think of myself in that way. My final copy could compare with anyone's. My errors were forgiven in advance, that is, before the document was printed out, through electronic correction. So in Christ we no longer bear the self identity of sinner.

> Therefore, my friends, since we have confidence to enter the sanctuary by the blood of Jesus, by the new and living way that he opened for us through the curtain (that is, through his flesh), and since we have a great priest over the house of God, let us approach with a true heart in full assurance of faith, with our hearts sprinkled clean from an evil conscience and our bodies washed with pure water (Heb. 10:19-22).

The main implication of the cross for the believer is that the message of Christ should be attended with the utmost seriousness (Heb. 2:14). Even this day an evil and unbelieving heart should be put away and sin rejected (Heb. 3:12-15). The believer should go on to perfection not perpetually retracing earlier steps (Heb. 6:1-4). Believers should approach

Christ with confidence, and overthrowing their spiritual doldrums, return to their active participation in him. They need to keep their eyes on the one who resisted unto death, and hold him up as a model (Heb. 12:3-7). They should be back on the road again to the heavenly Jerusalem.

> **Therefore lift your drooping hands and strengthen your weak knees, and make straight paths for your feet, so that what is lame may not be put out of joint, but rather be healed (Heb. 12:12-13).**

And just as Jesus died outside the camp, so too should the believer. "Let us then go to him outside the camp and bear the abuse he endured" (Heb. 13:13).

The death of Jesus was an inimitable moment in the life of God. It was once for all.

But looked at from the human perspective, those who follow the crucified Lord set out daily to emulate what he did, that is, they take up the cross daily.

# Questions for Discussion

1. Do Matthew, Mark and Luke reflect much on the significance of Christ's death? Why or why not?

2. Why did the disciples in Mark resist Christ's talk of his own death?

3. What did Jesus give as the explanation for his death at the time of the last supper?

4. Did Caiaphas understand Christ's death for the nation?

5. Why did Jesus wash the disciples feet?

6. Can disciples be accepted without being washed by Jesus?

7. How is Christ's death viewed as (a) sacrificial, (b) redemptive, and (c) reconciling?

8. Does the death of Christ have cosmic significance?

9. In what ways does the cross have bearing upon the believer's life, according to Paul?

10. What is the truth of the Gospel?

11. Why was Christ's sacrifice superior to any that preceded it in Hebrews?

12. Characterize a life lived in view of the cross in Hebrews.

# 8
# He Was Raised for Our Justification

*P*aul in Romans wrote of Jesus, "who was handed over to death for our trespasses and was raised for our justification" (4:25). In the sermon to Cornelius and his household Peter stated, "They put him to death by hanging him on a tree; but God raised him on the third day and allowed him to appear  . . ." (Acts 10:39-40).

The cross and the resurrection are different sides of the same coin. The cross is significant because the one dying there arose from the tomb. Many governments in the ancient Mediterranean world crucified political enemies, criminals, and insurrectionists. Thousands were punished and humiliated through death on a cross. It is unlikely that the memory of Jesus hanging there would have survived had not God raised him from the dead. The death of Jesus was different from any before or since on three counts: (1) The one who died was the Son of God, (2) He died on behalf of humankind, and (3) God raised him from the dead.

The resurrection was an event in the life of God himself, inasmuch as God himself was involved. "This Jesus God raised up" (Acts 2:32). In John, Jesus (the Word who was God) raised himself. "I lay down my life in order to take it up again. No one takes it from me, but I lay it down of my own accord. I have power to lay it down, and I have power to take it up again" (John 10:17-18). It was because of the resurrection that who Jesus was from the beginning later became obvious. For a little while he was lower than the angels (Heb. 2:9). For a time he voluntarily became human, taking on the form of a servant (Phil. 2:7). It was not immediately obvious who he was. "He was in the world, . . . yet the world did not know him" (John 1:10). Even the disciples took a long time to affirm his status as from God. But the resurrection erased all doubts. So Peter boldly professed to a great crowd of Jews assembled in Jerusalem on the feast of Pentecost: "Therefore let the entire house of Israel know with certainty that God has made him both Lord and Messiah, this Jesus whom you crucified" (Acts 2:36). God is himself life, and the giver of life. "Who gives life to the dead and calls into existence the things that do not exist" (Rom. 4:17). Jesus rose from the dead. He was God, so death had no hold over him. "But God raised him up, having freed him from death, because it was impossible for him to be held in its power" (Acts 2:24).

The resurrection is likewise an event in the life of believers when they receive Jesus Christ. Though often in Christian teaching the basis of salvation is focused upon the cross, Paul declared justification was dependent upon both the crucifixion and the resurrection. Jesus was "handed over to death for our trespasses and was raised for our justification" (Rom. 4:25). The resurrection of Christ has more far-reaching implications for the Christian walk than many have recognized. The resurrection is a preeminent event in the believer's life. It marks a turning point. "Therefore we have been buried with him by baptism into death, so that, just as Christ was raised from the dead by the glory of the Father, so we too might walk in newness of life" (Rom. 6:4). Because of his resurrection we "seek the things that are above, where Christ is, seated at the right hand of God" (Col. 3:1).

## *With Fear and Great Joy*

The synoptics predict the resurrection, they depict the circumstances surrounding it, but they do little theological reflection upon it, much as with the cross. Jesus spoke of his resurrection four times in the Gospel according to Matthew. The first occasion was his visit to Caesarea Philippi with the disciples. It was there that Peter declared to those surrounding Jesus, "You are the Messiah, the Son of the living God" (Matt. 16:16). After this confession Jesus began to teach his disciples about his death and resurrection. "From that time on, Jesus began to show his disciples that he must go to Jerusalem and undergo great suffering at the hands of the elders and chief priests and scribes, and be killed, and on the third day be raised" (Matt. 16:21; also 17:9,23).

Matthew alone reported the unusual occurrence of an earthquake shattering the tombs upon Jesus' death. After some hours on the cross Jesus cried with a loud voice and breathed his last (Matt. 27:50). Then two unprecedented events transpired. First, the curtain of the temple was torn in two from top to bottom. This was no doubt a show of the manner in which Christ in himself brought about unobstructed accessibility to God. In the second, an earthquake of great magnitude shook the earth. Rocks were split and the tombs were exposed. Many saints (that is, persons who had lived for God) arose from the dead. They milled around the tombs until Jesus was raised, then they entered Jerusalem and appeared to several persons (Matt. 27:53). We are not told exactly why these dead ones came to life. The first implication seems to be that the resurrection of the saints foreshadows the exhibition of God's capability in the resurrection of Jesus. God initiates life-giving force to raise Jesus, and his power is so potent that it spills over upon those in the tombs near the city. This unprecedented return to life seems also to anticipate the resurrection of all believers at the end time. The severing of the temple curtain makes clear that the resurrection of Jesus destroys whatever partitions prevent humans from worshiping God, and at the same time shatters those stone barriers which obstruct God's life-sustaining capabilities.

The resurrection of Jesus Christ shows that God has established a beachhead. The war is not over by any means. Many fierce battles are yet to be fought. Many persons have died since the resurrection of Christ. Many more are yet to die. But death no longer hampers hope. The Son of God has won a strategic victory over death. In Revelation a scroll appeared in the right hand of the one seated on a throne. An angel with a mighty voice called out for someone to open the scroll. But no one in heaven or on earth was worthy. The one who received the vision began to weep because the contents of the scroll could not be known. "Then one of the elders said to me, 'Do not weep. See, the Lion of the tribe of Judah, the Root of David, has conquered, so that he can open the scroll and its seven seals'" (Rev. 5:5). Jesus wrestled a mighty victory over death. By his victory he declared in word and deed that death is not the end. Life is available even beyond the grave for all who believe. With Christ's premier victory, we are confident that others will follow. God in this specific concrete act in the resurrection of Jesus Christ, has taken us aside and shown us a preview of the future. What a warm glow overpowers our lives; a great joy — deep and abiding!

As to the details of the resurrection we will follow Matthew's narrative. After Jesus' death, Joseph of Arimathea took the body of Jesus and laid it in his own new tomb and rolled a great stone across the opening (Matt. 27:59). The chief priests entreated Pilate to seal the tomb, which he did. The Sabbath passed, and early the next morning Mary

Magdalene and the other Mary made their way to the tomb. According to Mark, the women "brought spices so that they might go and anoint him" (Mark 16:1). The women went to the tomb to anoint a dead body. As they arrived, an earthquake hit, the stone was rolled away, and an angel sat on the stone. The soldiers drew back in great fear. The angel spoke to the women, "Do not be afraid; I know that you are looking for Jesus who was crucified. He is not here; for he has been raised, as he said. Come, see the place where he lay" (Matt. 28:5-6). Jesus had spoken with his followers more than once about his resurrection, but it had not registered. A dead person coming back to life was so incredible that they didn't really entertain it. If the women accepted Jesus' word for it, why did they come bearing spices? They did not anticipate a resurrected Christ, but with these unusual occurrences and the declaration of the angel, they now believed the impossible. "So they left the tomb quickly with fear and great joy, and ran to tell his disciples" (Matt. 28:8).

In the 1960s we lived in central Pennsylvania. All our bedrooms were on the second floor of a colonial. One night a shrill scream woke me from a dead sleep. Our oldest daughter insisted that there was a man in the hall. About half asleep I rose from the bed, went to the door and looked down the hall. I was awake almost immediately because at first glance I saw the man myself. I froze. My heart pounded wildly. But on second glance I could see that it wasn't a man, but the shadow of a man. I went to the bedroom cautiously to determine why the shadow was there. Dorothy used that room for ironing. She had ironed a shirt, placed it on a hanger and hung it on the door. We kept a lamp on in that room on the floor as a night light. The light shining on the shirt sent a shadow into the hall, which to all appearances was that of a man. In my first look I anticipated seeing a man and I did.

The women did not foresee the stone rolled away, an angel delivering a message, or an empty tomb. They went to anoint a dead body. What they discovered at the tomb therefore was not because of anticipation. It is difficult to explain the change that came over the women, or over the other discouraged and disoriented disciples, unless the tomb was, in fact, empty and no alternative explanation was forthcoming. Because the impossible had occurred, they experienced great fear and great joy. A person, who beyond the shadow of a doubt died, was alive. What a mind-boggling turn of affairs. The unanticipated actually transpired. Unlimited joy overpowered their thoughts. From this time on those who had witnessed the empty tomb were often reluctant witnesses. We have no record that persons who saw the risen Christ ever changed their story in subsequent years. Rather, we hear of them undergoing persecution and death, but no one recanted. Celsus, in the second century, assembled all the negative arguments he could muster against Christianity, but he included no incidents of the first witnesses recanting.

## *I Am the Resurrection and the Life*

In the Gospel of John, theological reflection on the resurrection, as was also true of the crucifixion, came early. "In him was life, and the life was the light of all people" (John 1:4). Because of his death and resurrection, "Everyone who believes in him may not perish but may have eternal life" (John 3:16). "Whoever believes in the Son has eternal life" (John 3:36). To the woman at the well Jesus declared that, "The water that I will give will become in them a spring of water gushing up to eternal life" (John 4:14). When those who accepted the teaching of Jesus believed his word they received a new consignment — for life everlasting. Such life begins here and now. But it is not yet complete. It wells up to eternal life.

The view that believers are from the first on the route to eternal life is found in the statements to the Samaritan woman, to the Jews in Jerusalem, and to Martha, the sister of Lazarus. To those in Jerusalem, Jesus declared, "Very truly, I tell you, anyone who hears my word and believes him who sent me has eternal life, and does not come under judgment, but has passed from death to life" (John 5:24). When one believes, eternal life sets in. It is never withdrawn as long as belief continues. The one who believes only knows life from now on. Because of faith in Christ, life is a fulfilled life. "I came that they may have life, and have it abundantly" (John 10:10). Death still arrives even for the one who believes. But immediately, upon resurrected consciousness, the believer apprehends life again. All that is known is life and that eternal.

Jesus made the same point in a discussion with Martha upon the death of her brother, Lazarus. Lazarus was ill and at death's door. His sisters Mary and Martha sent an urgent message to Jesus. Jesus received the communication, but did not immediately depart for Bethany. He told his disciples that the death of Lazarus was to be to God's glory (John 11:4). Two days later Jesus left for Bethany, knowing that in the meantime Lazarus had died. By the time he arrived, Lazarus had been in the tomb for four days. Martha met Jesus first. She told him that if he had come earlier her brother would be alive. She did not anticipate a resurrection (John 11:21). Jesus told her, "Your brother will rise again" (John 11:23). Martha replied that she knew he would arise in the final resurrection. Jesus, however, meant here and now and boldly declared, "I am the resurrection and the life. Those who believe in me, even though they die, will live, and everyone who lives and believes in me will never die" (John 11:25-26). Notice the claim. Those who believe will know only life, even though they die, in the sense that they will never experience a time gap in their existence. Immediately upon the experience of death, they will know life again. The grounds for life beyond the grave is not anything a human being possesses. Life beyond the grave is what Jesus grants upon belief in him. Death could not restrain Jesus, Son of God, just as it could not restrain Lazarus upon Jesus' loud pronouncement, "Lazarus, come out!" (John 11:43). Lazarus came out, with strips of cloth winding around and trailing his body.

## So All Will Be Made Alive in Christ

The most complete statement by Paul on the resurrection is found in 1 Corinthians 15. First, Paul declared that the gospel is that Christ died and was buried and "that he was raised on the third day in accordance with the Scriptures" (1 Cor. 15:3-4). Then he listed those who saw Christ raised. For Paul the support for a resurrected Christ was the testimony of those who were confronted by him after his death. The proof for his resurrection was the same as that of any other historical event. Such proof is based upon testimony, not scientific experimentation. "Scientific proof" consists of replicating the phenomenon. We can ourselves mix chemicals in a test tube to determine whether we get the same compound as alleged in Bombay. How can we crucify Christ anew to see if he will rise again? His unmerited death was a once-for-all event. We are dependent upon witnesses and the aftermath to set aside our doubts. Paul produced the witnesses. By the time he wrote, several had already died with the conviction that they saw the resurrected Christ. As I said before, no one, not even the enemies of early Christianity, knew of anyone who later reported or wrote out a retraction. The witnesses, according to Paul, were Cephas (Peter), the twelve, then five hundred men and women, then James, the brother of the Lord, then all the apostles (Paul labeled anyone who saw the risen Lord "apostle" and therefore designated to witness about the resurrection) and last of all to Paul himself (1 Cor. 15:4-9). Paul described himself as "untimely born." To all the other witnesses Jesus appeared before his ascension. It was only to Paul that he appeared from heaven (Acts 9:3-6).

Some at Corinth asserted that there is no resurrection from the dead. Apparently, they did not deny the resurrection of Christ. They denied human resurrection. "There is no resurrection of the dead" (1 Cor. 15:12). It may be, as was typical in Greece, that they did not deny the continuing existence of the human psyche. Plato believed that the soul is immortal. By that he claimed that souls of both humans and animals have always been and will always be. He believed that the continuation of life beyond the grave resided in something humans possess, that is, the soul. The immortal soul for Plato was trapped in an endless cycle of reincarnation. For most, reincarnation is bad news since sins are retained, and life succeeds guilt-ridden life. Only those few who embrace philosophy break the vicious cycle and join the immortal gods.

Paul, in contrast argued that immortal life resides in God alone. God raised Christ victorious from the grave. "We testified of God that he raised Christ" (1 Cor. 15:15). The resurrection of Christ guarantees that God has the power to raise from the dead those who believe in Christ. "For if the dead are not raised, then Christ has not been raised. If Christ has not been raised, your faith is futile and you are still in your sins" (1 Cor. 15:16-17). God in Christ broke the vicious cycle, if in fact there is such a cycle, which Paul denied. God raised Christ from the dead to die no more. Those who believe in him likewise break out of the cycle. Their sins are forgiven. They are no longer doomed to continue an abhorrent reoccurrence of sin-stained lives. "But in fact Christ has been raised from the dead, the first fruits of those who have died" (1 Cor. 15:20).

In the resurrection, the dead do not enter into either their old or a new body of flesh and blood (1 Cor. 15:50). Neither do they appear resurrected as bodiless souls or spirits.

**For in this tent we groan, longing to be clothed with our heavenly dwelling — if indeed, when we have taken it off we will not be found**

> naked. For while we are still in this tent, we groan under our burden, because we wish not to be unclothed but to be further clothed, so that what is mortal may be swallowed up by life (2 Cor. 5:2-4).

While the Greeks assumed that the ideal existence was the soul freed from the body, Paul was utterly threatened at the prospect of a bodiless existence. "We wish not to be unclothed, but to be further clothed." The new human state upon being resurrected is still bodily, but not the body of flesh and blood. "What is sown is perishable, what is raised is imperishable. It is sown in dishonor, it is raised in glory. It is sown in weakness, it is raised in power. It is sown a physical body, it is raised a spiritual body" (1 Cor. 15:42-44). It is a heavenly body, the same as the resurrected body of Christ. "Just as we have borne the image of the man of dust, we will also bear the image of the man of heaven" (1 Cor. 15:49). It is upon resurrection that humans become immortal. "For this perishable body must put on imperishability, and this mortal body must put on immortality" (1 Cor. 15:53).

Paul believed that at the coming again, Christ and those who are his will enter the realm of God as a group. "But in fact Christ has been raised from the dead, the first fruits of those who have died. . . . But each in his own order: Christ the first fruits, then at his coming those who belong to Christ" (1 Cor. 15:20,23). "For since we believe that Jesus died and rose again, even so, through Jesus, God will bring with him those who have died" (1 Thess. 4:14).

A popular view is that persons will stand in line so as to present their credentials for entry into heaven one at a time, just as if passing through immigration to visit a foreign country. But that is not Paul's conception. He believed that Christ himself will vouch for the right of all gathered by him to enter as a group.

In 1984 we entered Communist China at the Shanghai airport as members of a People-to-People Tour. This is the only entry we have ever made into a foreign country, requiring a document check, that let us come in as a group. Our tour leader collected all our passports and visas, as well as our luggage. These were then verified and checked by the officials as we remained together. When the immigration officers were satisfied, we walked through the checkpoint together without stopping. In the same manner Paul depicted the entry of believers with Christ into heaven. We will not have to worry as to whether our papers will check out. He will vouch for all who are his.

## *The Resurrection as an Event in the Life of the Believer*

We have already noticed that the resurrection provides a new outlook on the future for the believer. Because of Christ's victory over death, death can never be viewed again in the same way. On June 6, 1944, the allied forces of British, Canadian, and U.S. troops under General Dwight D. Eisenhower, invaded Normandy Beach. A beachhead was established by this notable offensive under the cryptic label, D-Day. At that point the war could never be viewed again in the same manner. It was not that the war was over. General Patton still rumbled around in tanks in France, the Low Lands, and Germany. D-Day was not V-E (victory in Europe) Day. V-E Day did not occur until May 8, 1945. World War II ended on August 14, 1945, V-J (victory over Japan) Day, after the bombing of Hiroshima and Nagasaki. But once a beachhead was established at Normandy, the war could not be viewed in the same way again. Whatever the battles still yet to be fought, victory was assured. Because of the resurrection of Jesus Christ death can never be viewed the same for those who believe. His conquest of death assures our victory!

The resurrection of Jesus also assures that his generation, as well as all later generations, will go forth in ministry empowered by the risen Lord. At the ending of Matthew

Jesus declared: "And remember, I am with you always, to the end of the age" (Matt. 28:20).

Because the Lord has arisen, the earthly ministry of Jesus continues. "And they went out and proclaimed the good news everywhere, while the Lord worked with them and confirmed the message by the signs that accompanied it" (Mark 16:20). Luke puts it a somewhat different way. The resurrected Jesus continued to be present with the disciples. After arising from the grave he assembled with the disciples at table (Luke 22:16). At the table the eyes of the disciples are opened, and they recognize that it is Jesus who has blessed the bread (Luke 24:31). And Jesus will continue to be present whenever his disciples break the bread. Upon the disciples Jesus conferred his powers in respect to forgiving sins (John 20:23) and his mission of feeding the sheep (John 21:17). They continued his work on earth.

The resurrection also has implications for the life of the believer individually. Individuals are empowered by Christ's resurrection, however, not so much for their own needs, but for the needs of the larger body of believers. The risen Christ gives gifts to believers, but they are to be employed for the welfare of the body (Eph. 4:7,12-13). The new gifts of these believers are not for self-aggrandizement, but for Christ and his body. "And he died for all, so that those who live might live no longer for themselves, but for him who died and was raised for them" (2 Cor. 5:15).

Paul in Romans extolled the freedom from sin possible through the death of Christ. At the same time he characterized the new sanctified life as drawing on the power of the resurrection. Having died with Christ through the cross, the believer is also raised for a new life. "Therefore we have been buried with him by baptism into death, so that, just as Christ was raised from the dead by the glory of the Father, so we too might walk in newness of life" (Rom. 6:4). The resurrection has implications for the future. "For if we have been united with him in a death like his, we will certainly be united with him in a resurrection like his" (Rom. 6:5). But also here and now life in Christ is modeled after the resurrection. "So you also must consider yourselves dead to sin and alive to God in Christ Jesus" (Rom. 6:11). A new life style is evident. "So if anyone is in Christ, there is a new creation: everything old has passed away; see, everything has become new! All this is from God, who reconciled us to himself through Christ, and has given us the ministry of reconciliation" (2 Cor. 5:17-18).

In Ephesians and Colossians the resurrection of Christ, when appropriated by the believers, goes a long way toward elevating them on a new plain above ordinary human existence. In Christ's ascension God "seated him at his right hand in the heavenly places" (*epouranios*, Eph. 1:20). Believers receive "every spiritual blessing in the heavenly places" (Eph. 1:3). Likewise they are elevated with Christ and seated in the same place. "And raised us up with him and seated us with him in the heavenly places in Christ Jesus" (Eph. 2:6). Rulers and authorities occupy the same *epouranios* (Eph. 3:10), and at least some of these are "cosmic powers of this present darkness, against the spiritual forces of evil in the heavenly places" (Eph. 6:12). Believers exist in the new realm of Christ, but the stakes are higher in terms of the surrounding powers, for they too are more potent. But as a result of the resurrection believers "will be able to quench all the flaming arrows of the evil one" (Eph. 6:16).

Because of the resurrection of Jesus Christ believers give their attention to the ways of heaven. "So if you have been raised with Christ, seek the things that are above, where Christ is, seated at the right hand of God. Set your minds on things that are above, not on things that are on earth, for you have died, and your life is hidden with Christ in God" (Col. 3:1-3). The things above have to do with love, kindness, meekness. "Above all, clothe yourselves with love, which binds everything together in perfect harmony. And let the peace of Christ rule in your hearts, to which indeed you were called in the one body. And be thankful" (Col. 3:12-13). His love truly compels the believer.

The resurrection of Jesus Christ brings new life to the believer now and a preview of what is to come. His resurrection is already an event for all believers, but even more it will be the grandest of all historical moments at their final and nonrescindable resurrection.

# Questions for Discussion

1. What was different about Christ's death on a cross from that of all others who so died?

2. In what way was the resurrection an experience in the life of God?

3. What is the implication of the opening of the graves when Christ died?

4. Did the women go to Christ's tomb anticipating seeing a raised Lord?

5. What is the implication of Jesus' being the resurrection and the life?

6. Why did the Corinthians claim there was no resurrection from the dead?

7. What did Paul mean when he argued for a bodily resurrection?

8. Should Christians believe that when they were born they were given immortal souls?

9. Will Christians after death enter heaven by themselves, and one at a time?

10. Will the body raised be one of flesh?

11. What are the implications of the resurrection of Jesus for the continuing earthly ministry of Jesus?

12. What are the characteristics of the newly resurrected life that begins at baptism?

# 9
# They Went Forth as Witnesses

*D*id it ever occur to you that Jesus spent almost all his thirty-some years in one small country, that is, ancient Palestine? If Jesus really came to win humanity to God, why did he reach out to so few? Why didn't he travel widely? Why didn't he undertake a speaking tour through Asia and cross the Bering Straits into the Americas? Why didn't he take a boat to Athens, Rome, and Madrid? Or better still, why didn't he float grandiosely above every part of the globe so as to be seen by all of humankind, even those in the remotest of parts? The answer lies in the preparing and nurturing of witnesses. Once ready, they were assigned the task of traversing the world. "And he said to them, 'Go into all the world and proclaim the good news to the whole creation'" (Mark 16:15).

In his sermon to the household of Cornelius Peter assigned an imperative role to those who saw the risen Christ. "We are witnesses to all that he did both in Judea and in Jerusalem. They put him to death by hanging him on a tree; but God raised him on the third day" (Acts 10:39-40). Jesus did not set out to touch as many people as possible. He worked with, and after his death appeared to, especially those who were to proclaim who he was and what his mission was. They were selected and consigned to be witnesses. God desired that everyone hear of his unspeakable gift. The good news was to be scattered abroad by those who accompanied Jesus in his ministry and talked with the risen Christ. God himself planned it that Jesus would cover little of the earth and rub shoulders with only a few even in that land.

The role of witnesses is developed in two main places in the New Testament, in Luke-Acts and in the Gospel of John. Paul, in addition, wrote of the gospel proclaimed by those sent, that is, apostles.

## *You Are Witnesses of These Things*

Luke prepared his two-volume account of early Christianity in order that those who read them, though never having seen or heard of Jesus, might nevertheless be introduced to the truth of his person and message. He read the reports of some of those who were present, and interviewed others, "those who from the beginning were eyewitnesses and servants of the word . . . so that you may know the truth concerning the things about which you have been instructed" (Luke 1:2,4). Just before his ascension Jesus emphasized how those who had been with him for these many months would serve as witnesses of his life and teachings. "You are witnesses of these things. And see, I am sending upon you what my Father promised; so stay here in the city until you have been clothed with power from on high" (Luke 24:48-49). Once the disciples received the power from on high, they were to be witnesses in concentric circles from Jerusalem until they traversed the globe. "You will be my witnesses in Jerusalem, in all Judea and Samaria, and to the ends of the earth" (Acts 1:8). In fact, the book of Acts may be outlined according to the gospel proclamation in these progressively wider circles: in Jerusalem, Acts 1–7; in all Judea and Samaria, Acts 8–12; and to the ends of the earth, Acts 13–28.

The twelve were a special group of witnesses. In Acts also the term "apostle" (that is, "one sent") normally refers to the twelve, except that in Acts 14:14 Barnabas and Paul are so designated. "When the apostles Barnabas and Paul heard of it . . . ." In order to be among the twelve, according to Acts 1:21, when a replacement was being sought for Judas, one had to have been in the group that accompanied the Lord "beginning from the baptism of John until the day when he was taken up from us" (v. 22). But clearly additional persons were perceived as witnesses including perhaps all the one hundred and twenty men and woman mentioned in Acts 1:15. Paul declared to those at the synagogue in Antioch of Pisidia, after setting out details about the death of Jesus, "But God raised him from the dead, and for many days he appeared to those who came up with him from Galilee to Jerusalem, and they are now his witnesses to the people" (Acts 13:30-31). Luke took pains to note that women were included among those who came to Jerusalem. "But all his acquaintances, including the women who had followed him from Galilee, stood at a distance, watching these things" (Luke 23:49). As Joseph of Arimathea took Jesus to his rock-hewn tomb, "The women who had come with him [Jesus] from Galilee followed, and they saw the tomb and how his body was laid" (Luke 23:55). Again in Acts 1:14 Luke singled out the women: "All these [that is the eleven] were constantly devoting themselves to prayer, together with certain women, including Mary the mother of Jesus, as well as his brothers." It was therefore these numerous witnesses who were prepared by God through what they had seen and heard, who now were poised to carry the story about Jesus to the ends of the earth.

Those designated as witnesses clearly were ready to function as God planned, because they could tell in detail the story of what Jesus said and did. The special focus of their witness is to be that Jesus was raised from the dead. This point is made frequently in Luke-Acts. Luke ends his Gospel by pointing out that the law of Moses, the prophets, and the psalms predicted "that the Messiah is to suffer and to rise from the dead on the third day" (Luke 24:46). The witness of the disciples therefore pinpointed this mighty work of God. "You are witnesses of these things" (Luke 24:48). The replacement for Judas took on this special role in that he was to "become a witness with us [the eleven] to his resurrection" (Acts 1:22). Those from among the believers who addressed the crowds on the feast of Pentecost, according to Peter could testify that "Jesus God raised up," so "that all of us are witnesses" (Acts 2:32). Later Peter and John daily addressed crowds at the temple, and central to their message was "You killed the Author of life, whom God raised from the dead. To this we are witnesses" (Acts 3:15). On another occasion the high priest had the apostles arrested and thrown in prison. But even though the officials did not release them, they showed up again at the temple steps teaching. So once again the high priest confronted them and asked why they were preaching even though they were prohibited from doing so. Peter and John told them, "The God of our ancestors raised up Jesus, whom you had killed by hanging him on a tree. God exalted him at his right hand as Leader and Savior that he might give repentance to Israel and forgiveness of sins. And we are witnesses to these things . . ." (Acts 5:30-32). Paul also spoke to the risen Lord so knew first hand of his resurrection. As a result he took his place as a witness to the resurrection along with the rest. "The God of our ancestors has chosen you to know his will, to see the Righteous One and to hear his own voice; for you will be his witness to all the world of what you have seen and heard" (Acts 22:14-15; also 26:16).

These early witnesses spoke not so much of what God had done specifically for them as individuals, but what Jesus had accomplished for all of humankind by his death and his resurrection. He overcame sin and death, and through this action of God is able to forgive the sins of all those who come to him, and also offer the assurance of a resurrected life beyond the grave. The common word for "witness" in Greek was, in the noun form, *martys* and, in the verb form, *martyreo*, the latter word also being sometimes translated "testify." The relation of this word to the English word "martyr" is obvious. As yet in New Testament times, *martys* did not commonly imply a witness which one made by dying for what one believed, though this meaning is obvious in Acts 22:20 in the New International Version. Later in the first century, Christians died for their convictions about Christ. They therefore witnessed even though it resulted in death. According to the later traditions many of the twelve were martyred because of their testimony about the risen Christ.

## *Sent from God*

In the Gospel of John, multiple testimonies point to Jesus as one sent from God. "The works that the Father has given me to complete, the very works that I am doing, testify on my behalf that the Father has sent me" (John 5:36).

The first witness was John the Baptist. "He came as a witness to testify to the light, so that all might believe through him" (John 1:7). He testified that he was not the Messiah, but was a servant, preparing the way of the Lord (that is, the Messiah) (John 1:19-23). To his disciples, John testified in regard to Jesus, "Here is the Lamb of God who takes away the sin of the world!" (John 1:29). Furthermore, "I myself have seen and have testified that this is the Son of God" (John 1:34).

It is particularly in John 5 that the testimony pointing to Jesus as sent from God is set out. Jesus, in keeping with Jewish rules, stated that if he testified about himself it would not stand (John 5:31). One needs other testimonies, not self-attestations. The status of Jesus is therefore dependent on the testimonies of others. The significance of testimonies is developed also in John 8. "Then the Pharisees said to him 'You are testifying on your own behalf; your testimony is not valid.' Jesus answered, 'Even if I testify on my own behalf, my testimony is valid because I know where I have come from and where I am going . . .'" (John 8:13-14). Jesus then declared that his judgment was not singular, but it was also the judgment of "the Father who sent me" (John 8:16). The law, in this regard, Jesus stated, is that "'the testimony of two witnesses is valid. I testify on my own behalf, and the Father who sent me testifies on my behalf'" (John 8:17-18).

In John 5, Jesus set forth four different testimonies. First, John the Baptist testified to the truth. But there is another testimony that is greater than that of John. This second testimony is "The works that the Father has given me to complete, the very works that I am doing, testify on my behalf that the Father has sent me" (John 5:36; also 10:25, 12:17). Third, he mentioned that the Father by speaking also testified on his behalf. He observed to the Jews, however, that they had not heard God's voice (John 5:37). What did Jesus have in mind? Apparently he had reference to the words God spoke to John about Jesus when the Spirit descended upon him from heaven like a dove (John 1:32). John reported, "I myself did not know him, but the one who sent me to baptize with water said to me, 'He on whom you see the Spirit descend and remain is the one who baptizes with the Holy Spirit'" (John 1:33). Fourth, the Scriptures testify as to Jesus' identity. "You search the scriptures because you think that in them you have eternal life; and it is they that testify on my behalf" (John 5:39).

In addition, the Holy Spirit witnessed as to Christ's person. "When the Advocate comes, whom I will send to you from the Father, the Spirit of Truth who comes from the Father, he will testify on my behalf" (John 15:26). The disciples themselves also become a witness. "You also are to testify because you have been with me from the beginning" (John 15:27; 19:35; 21:24).

In John's perspective many pointers identified Jesus as sent from God. The works of Jesus of which he spoke were highlighted in the many signs Jesus performed. Once again witnessing, as set forth in the Gospel of John, was not so much some personal, individual way in which God made known his acceptance. Rather it was the testimony in statements and action which made it clear beyond reasonable doubt that Jesus was the only begotten Son of God.

## *As to One Untimely Born*

Paul seldom employed the words "witness" or "testimony" in regard to the verification of Jesus as Lord, but he certainly believed that special persons were prepared so as to carry the good news to every creature under heaven. His commitment is especially clear as he closes Romans.

> **For I will not venture to speak of anything except what Christ has accomplished through me to win obedience from the Gentiles, by word and deed, by the power of signs and wonders, by the power of the Spirit of God, so that from Jerusalem and as far around as Illyricum I have fully proclaimed the good news of Christ (Rom. 15:18-19).**

So who were these witnesses? Interestingly Paul did not mention women specifically by category or name, but the Gospels all reported that women saw the risen Christ, and in some cases, that they were the first to do so. In Paul's list, the resurrected Jesus first appeared to Cephas, that is Peter. Then he appeared to the twelve. Somewhat later he appeared to above 500 brothers at the same time most of whom were alive, but some had died (1 Cor. 15:6). Next he appeared to James, presumably the brother of Jesus, and then to all the apostles. In this last remark Paul employed the term "apostle" in the more generic sense of "one sent," rather than in the more specific sense of "The Twelve." We know that Paul used the term generically because he identified James the brother of the Lord as an apostle (Gal. 1:19), as well as certain Jews at Rome. "Greet Andronicus and Junia, my relatives who were in prison with me; they are prominent among the apostles, and they were in Christ before I was" (Rom. 16:7). I think the best conclusion is that Andronicus and Junia were husband and wife, parallel with Prisca and Aquila (Rom. 16:3), though this is disputed. It is interesting that Paul did not disqualify the super "apostles," who arrived at Corinth and were mentioned in 2 Corinthians, on the grounds that they had not seen the risen Lord. It is very doubtful that these who arrived, however, and caused the trouble, were among the twelve. Paul challenged their style of apostleship, not their firsthand witness.

We are now ready to take up Paul's own situation. Here and elsewhere he includes himself in the category of apostles (Gal. 1:1; 2 Cor. 1:1). How did he conceive his own status? Clearly he was not a thirteenth added to the twelve. The more than five hundred were "apostles" as well as whatever additional numbers saw the risen Lord (1 Cor. 15:7). The visitors in 2 Corinthians could have been in the latter group. Paul declared himself to be different than all the rest. "As to one untimely born, he appeared also to me" (1 Cor. 15:8). His statement implies, without doubt, that all these others mentioned saw the risen Lord before he ascended. Paul saw the risen Lord, but on the road to Damascus. The appearance was from heaven, where Jesus is situated at the right hand of God (Rom. 8:34). Paul did not know, it would seem, of anyone else to whom the risen Lord appeared after his ascension. Paul was one of a kind, and the end of a line. He was especially chosen, even though later, because of his mission to the Gentiles (Rom. 15:15-16). No other new ministry requiring an apostle was left to be opened.

Can believers in the Lord be his witnesses today? In some church groups there is constant talk of testifying, giving one's testimony, and of witnessing. It is clear that no one today has the qualifications for being among the twelve (Acts 1:21-22). Even Paul did not claim that privilege, though he claimed to be an apostle. Witnessing is certainly proper as long as the content is that of the first witnesses. That witness was that Christ died for all who will receive him and through his death sins are forgiven. Then because of his resurrection, in the end time believers will arise, just as Christ arose from the grave. The problem with current testimonials is that we tend to learn more about the person testifying than we do about the one sent from God. Paul refrained from boasting about whatever may have been Christ's special personal gift to him. "If I must boast, I will boast of the things that show my weakness" (2 Cor. 11:30).

The way in which the Good News spread because of this early witnessing is instructive. If the people of our generation are to hear that God sent his Son, and what he accomplished in his death and resurrection, it will be because we give our testimony to what he said and did. We have a witness. Our witness is that Jesus "was handed over to death for our trespasses and was raised for our justification" (Rom. 4:25).

# Questions for Discussion

1. Why did Jesus reach out to so few people?

2. What was the main witness of the qualified witnesses in Luke/Acts?

3. What were the qualifications for being among the Twelve?

4. What were the qualifications for the rest of the witnesses in Luke/Acts?

5. Were women included among the witnesses in Luke/Acts?

6. What was the Greek meaning of the word *martyr* in New Testament times? Of the English word "martyr"?

7. What is the focus of witnessing or testifying in John?

8. Who and what witnessed to Christ in John?

9. What did Paul mean when he wrote that he was "as one untimely born"?

10. Did Paul leave the door open for apostles in every age?

11. Did Paul use the term apostle to include more than the Twelve?

12. Should we give our testimony in the twenty-first century? If so, of what should it consist?

# 10
# His Ministry Continued under the Auspices of the Holy Spirit

The ministry of Jesus was Spirit anointed. "And when Jesus had been baptized, just as he came up from the water, suddenly the heavens were opened to him and he saw the Spirit of God descending like a dove and alighting on him" (Matt. 3:16). Jesus, in turn, is to anoint with the Holy Spirit those who take up his ministry. "He will baptize you with the Holy Spirit and fire" (Matt. 3:11).

According to the Gospel of John, Jesus did not bestow the Holy Spirit upon his disciples until after the resurrection. "Now he said this about the Spirit, which believers in him were to receive; for as yet there was no Spirit, because Jesus was not yet glorified" (John 7:39). On the evening of the resurrection, the disciples were meeting behind locked doors in fear of the Jewish officials. Jesus appeared in their midst. They saw his hands and his side.

> Jesus said to them again, "Peace be with you. As the Father has sent me, so I send you." When he had said this, he breathed on them and said to them, "Receive the Holy Spirit" (John 20:21-22).

No explicit statement may be found in the synoptics which infers that the disciples were spirit filled during the time of Jesus' ministry. Their power rather was derived from invoking the name of Jesus. "The seventy returned with joy, saying, 'Lord, in your name even the demons submit to us!" (Luke 10:17). The disciples were instructed by Jesus to wait in Jerusalem until they were endued with power from on high (Luke 24:49). The disciples received the Holy Spirit, that is, the baptism of the Holy Spirit, on the feast of Pentecost. "All of them were filled with the Holy Spirit and began to speak in other languages, as the Spirit gave them ability" (Acts 2:4). This special Holy Spirit baptism came to empower the apostolic ministry.

### Another Helper

In the Gospel of John the disciples are to continue the earthly ministry of Jesus assisted by the Holy Spirit in the same manner in which Jesus helped them while he was with them.

> And I will ask the Father, and he will give you another Advocate, to be with you forever. This is the Spirit of truth, whom the world cannot receive, because it neither sees him nor knows him. You know him, because he abides with you, and he will be in you (John 14:16-17).

Under the power of the Holy Spirit, according to Jesus, the disciples will be able to "do the works that I do and, in fact, will do greater works than these, because I am going to the Father" (John 14:12). It is difficult to know in what manner the magnitude of the works of the disciples exceeded those of Jesus, except that because of the expanding circle of disciples, the quantity increased exponentially. Jesus assured the disciples that it was to their advantage that he leave, so that he could send the Holy Spirit as a replacement.

> Nevertheless I tell you the truth: it is to your advantage that I go away, for if I do not go away, the Advocate will not come to you; but if I go, I will send him to you (John 16:7).

The Greek word translated "Advocate" in the NRSV is *parakletos*. The word literally means, "called to the side of." The sense is that such a person working aside another is an assistant or helper. Scholars have employed various English words to translate *parakletos*. Roman Catholic translations have tended to transliterate the Greek letters into the English as "Paraclete." The King James Version translated it "comforter." While the Holy Spirit does indeed comfort disciples of Jesus, the Spirit's work far exceeds that of comforting. The New International Version translated *parakletos* with the word "counselor." The Holy Spirit likewise serves as a counselor to the disciples, but that too is a limited aspect of his work. The NRSV's, "advocate" picks up on a more expanded aspect of the work of the Spirit in the lives of the disciples, but that too is limited. Both counselors and advocates tend to be perceived as professionals consulted when one is in trouble — counselors in schools and advocates in legal offices. While offering assistance in the day of crisis, the work of the Holy Spirit is much more comprehensive than that of a troubleshooter according to John. The Today's English Version and the Contemporary English Version translate *parakletos* "helper." It would seem to me that "helper" catches the wider aspects of the work of the Spirit and may therefore be the best translation. The word, however, seems a bit weak for the powerful role which the Holy Spirit plays in the lives of those who believe. Perhaps Divine Helper might better convey the sense of *parakletos*. In the final analysis, the significance of the term must be fleshed out through scrutinizing the manner in which the Holy Spirit empowers the disciples so as to further the earthly ministry of Jesus.

According to the Gospel of John, the Holy Spirit or Paraclete will: (1) enable the disciples to do greater works than Christ (14:12) and be with the disciples forever (14:16); (2) dwell with them and be in them: "You know him, because he abides with you, and he will be in you" (John 14:17); (3)

"teach you everything, and remind you of all that I have said to you" (John 14:26); (4) bear witness to Christ, and in turn enable the disciples to testify (John 15:26-27). He will also glorify Christ, "because he will take what is mine and declare it to you" (John 16:14); (5) "And when he comes, he will prove the world wrong about sin and righteousness and judgment" (John 16:8); and (6) "When the Spirit of truth comes, he will guide you into all the truth; for he will not speak on his own, but will speak whatever he hears, and he will declare to you the things that are to come" (John 16:13).

The Divine Helper, the Paraclete, will do far more than comfort, counsel, and advocate. He will empower believers to witness about the Christ, and bring unbelievers to conviction. He will remind them of what the earthly Christ taught. He will give them what additional truth is needed, including what is to transpire in the future. Some of these works of the Spirit may be limited to the early church leaders. But some of them are to continue forever since the Holy Spirit is to continue with all the disciples of Jesus forever. To help ascertain whether the *parakletos* only works through the twelve, Holy Spirit anointment in 1 John must be examined.

Much of the discussion of the Holy Spirit in 1 John has to do with those who left. "They went out from us, but they did not belong to us; for if they had belonged to us, they would have remained with us" (1 John 2:19). Those who left apparently claimed a special anointing of the Holy Spirit which conferred on them uncommon knowledge. They basked in their newly gained powers as compared with the pitiful run-of-the-mill believers left behind. John reassured the faithful believers, "But you have been anointed by the Holy One, and all of you have knowledge" (1 John 2:20). Furthermore,

> As for you, the anointing that you received from him abides in you, and so you do not need anyone to teach you. But as his anointing

teaches you about all things, and is true and is not a lie, and just as
it has taught you, abide in him (1 John 2:27).

Notice that these texts affirm that the ordinary members
in these presumably Asia Minor churches are declared to have
the same powers as set forth in John 14:26 and John 16:13.
So in the Johannine materials, the works of the Paraclete are
present in all believers, not just in the Twelve, so as to provide Divine Help in continuing the earthly ministry of Jesus
as long as time shall last.

The continuing presence of the spirit does not, however,
open the door to latter day "new revelations" that add to or
conflict with the apostolic word. The valid knowledge, John
asserted, had already been declared. Those claiming "new revelation" must be tested. "Beloved, do not believe every spirit, but test the spirits to see whether they are from God; for
many false prophets have gone out into the world" (1 John
4:1). Upon what grounds is the testing to be done? "We are
from God." John wrote. "Whoever knows God listens to us,
and whoever is not from God does not listen to us. From this
we know the spirit of truth and the spirit of error" (1 John
4:6). The truth, therefore, that believers in all ages possess,
that comes with Holy Spirit anointing, must be consistent
with the apostolic teaching which later was collected, forming
the New Testament.

## To the Ends of the Earth

In Luke-Acts the Holy Spirit was especially involved in
the opening up of ministries, those of John the Baptist, Jesus,
the apostolic ministry, the ministry to the Samaritans, and
the ministry to the Gentiles, that is, to the ends of the earth.

John the Baptist was "filled with the Holy Spirit" (Luke
1:15), so his ministry was Holy Spirit empowered. Jesus was
conceived by the Holy Spirit (Luke 2:35), and anointed by
the Holy Spirit so as to open up his ministry (Luke 3:22). As

Jesus launched his ministry at the synagogue in Nazareth, he read from the Isaiah scroll "The Spirit of the Lord is upon me," and thereby acknowledged the role of the Spirit (Luke 4:18). The disciples did not arbitrarily open up ministries on their own. They were to wait until "clothed with power from on high" (Luke 24:49).

In the book of Acts the outline of the whole is declared as describing the new ministries of the early church: (1) Jerusalem, (2) all Judea and Samaria, and (3) to the ends of the earth (Acts 1:8). Each of these ministries were opened with the descending of the Holy Spirit. The Holy Spirit, according to Luke-Acts, is a gift to all those baptized in the name of Jesus. They therefore have received Holy Spirit baptism. But the Holy Spirit descends with a special purpose when the ministries are opened up. Those are unique events. Once these ministries are opened, all the possible ministries are opened since the third is to the ends of the earth. These unique outpourings of the Holy Spirit are therefore not to be repeated.

The commencement of the ministry in Jerusalem is reported in Acts 2. This is the first special outpouring of the Spirit which occurred on the day of Pentecost. The one hundred twenty gathered in one place when divided tongues of fire descended on each of them. "All of them were filled with the Holy Spirit and began to speak in other languages, as the Spirit gave them ability" (Acts 2:4). The Holy Spirit empowered them and the speaking in tongues amazed the onlookers "because each one heard them speaking in the native language of each" (Acts 2:6).

The ministry was opened with the powerful descent of the Holy Spirit. The Spirit also was given to each of the three thousand baptized believers. The prediction of John the Baptist regarding the baptism of Jesus, "He will baptize you with the Holy Spirit" (Luke 3:16, Acts 11:16), began to happen to those baptized on Pentecost and later. According to Acts 2:38-39, "Repent, and be baptized every one of you in the name of Jesus Christ so that your sins may be forgiven; and you will receive the gift of the Holy Spirit. For the promise is for you, for your children, and for all who are far away, everyone whom the Lord our God calls to him." The gift of the Holy Spirit received at baptism is not just for the apostolic age, but for all ages to come.

The Greek word translated "gift" in Acts 2:39 is *dorea*. The word in its various forms may mean a singular gift. Some have argued that in Acts 2:39 the gift is the Spirit itself and does not imply spiritual gifts. Paul employs *dorea* in that manner though not in reference to the Holy Spirit, but to Christ himself (Rom. 5:15,17; 2 Cor. 9:15). At the same time Paul used *charisma* to refer to the gift of Christ himself (Romans 5:15,16; 6:23) showing that Paul used the words *dorea* and *charisma* interchangeably. *Doron*, from the same root, can mean gifts, for example, the three gifts of the Magi (Matt. 2:11), the gifts given at the temple (Luke 21:1), and in Hebrews the gifts offered by the priests (5:1; 8:3,4; 9:9; 11:4). So from the usage of the word itself one cannot insist that the promise of Acts 2:38,39 has to do with the indwelling of the Holy Spirit rather than the gifts of the Spirit. This is the case, even though Paul normally employed the word *charisma* when writing of the gifts of the Spirit (Rom. 12:6; 1 Cor. 12:4,9,30,31).

The ministry to Judea and Samaria commenced when a severe persecution was launched against the Christians in Jerusalem and Christians were scattered throughout the region. Philip, who was among the seven selected to minister to the needs of the Grecian widows (Acts 6:5), went to the city of Samaria and proclaimed the Messiah to them. Several among them were baptized. When the apostles heard of the successes, they sent Peter and John to Samaria. The Spirit had not as yet come upon the baptized there, but did when Peter and John prayed for them and laid their hands on them (Acts 8:15). In this case, however, no special manifestations are mentioned, perhaps because in a sense this was an extension of the Jerusalem ministry.

Saul, later Paul, met the ascended Lord (untimely, as he put it) on the way to Damascus where he sought to ferret out those who believed in Christ and force them to go to Jerusalem. Paul then was baptized and received the Holy Spirit (Acts 9:17,18). He then was told of his ministry (Acts 26:16-17). Paul, therefore, became the chief instrument of the Holy Spirit (Acts 13:2-4) to plant churches among the Gentiles.

From the Jerusalem perspective, however, it was Peter whom the Spirit of God employed to open the Gentile mission. One day at noon Peter, who had traveled to Joppa to be with believers, went on the housetop to pray. He had a vision of a sheet being let down from heaven filled with unclean animals. Peter was told to eat, but he refused on the grounds that he had never eaten anything profane or unclean (Acts 10:9-14). A voice said to him "What God has made clean, you must not call profane" (Acts 10:15). Peter was puzzled about what all of this meant when servants from Cornelius, a Roman centurion, asked for him. "While Peter was still thinking about the vision, the Spirit said to him, 'Look, three men are searching for you. Now get up, go down, and go with them without hesitation; for I have sent them'" (Acts 10:19-20). Upon arriving in Caesarea, Peter found a number of people assembled at Cornelius's house. He told them that God himself had told him to proclaim the story of Jesus to them (Acts 10:28). Then the Holy Spirit confirmed God's intentions both to Peter and those assembled (Acts 10:44-47).

Later, when reporting to the church in Jerusalem, Peter justified accepting these Gentiles as fellow believers because the same phenomena occurred as on the day of Pentecost because the Holy Spirit fell upon them also and they began to speak in tongues, in this case, both to convince Peter and other Jewish believers who heard the report, as well as the household of Cornelius and onlookers. As a result, Peter ordered them to be baptized (Acts 10:48). Back in Jerusalem, after being criticized for eating with the uncircumcised, Peter declared,

> And as I began to speak, the Holy Spirit fell upon them just as it had upon us at the beginning. And I remembered the word of the Lord, how he had said, "John baptized with water, but you will be baptized with the Holy Spirit." If then God gave them the same gift that he gave us when we believed in the Lord Jesus Christ, who was I that I could hinder God? (Acts 11:15-17).

It is important to note the language Peter employed as well his reference to the promise of John the Baptist.

The baptism of the Holy Spirit at Caesarea resulted in a specific gift of the Holy Spirit as at Pentecost, that is, speaking in tongues. Interestingly, however, when Peter declared that "God gave them the same gift that he gave us," the Greek word for "gift" is *dorea*, the same word Peter employed for the gift every believer is to receive in Acts 2:38,39. It is not clear, however, that Peter claimed that every believer will speak in tongues. No such phenomena is mentioned, for example, at Samaria (Acts 8:15-19). In another case, however, at Ephesus, Paul discovered a group who had been baptized into John's baptism and who had not even so much as heard of the Holy Spirit. After these people (approximately twelve of them) were baptized in the name of the Lord Jesus, Paul laid hands on them and they spoke in tongues and prophesied (Acts 19:1-7).

From examining Luke-Acts we therefore conclude that all those who believed in Christ after the day of Pentecost were baptized in or by the Holy Spirit. They were also baptized in water. Not all of them, however, spoke in tongues. This was reserved for the special occasions upon which the Holy Spirit opened new ministries. Not every believer later was to speak in tongues upon receiving the Holy Spirit. Once opened, the ministries in Jerusalem, Samaria and to the ends of the earth never needed to be reopened.

## A New Creation Is Everything

Paul believed that because of the death and resurrection of Jesus of Nazareth a new day dawned for humankind. Because of him a new creation was possible because of the arrival of the Spirit of God. Paul's vision may come from Ezekiel.

> A new heart I will give you, and a new spirit I will put within you; and I will remove from your body the heart of stone and give you a heart of flesh. I will put my spirit within you, and make you follow my statutes and be careful to observe my ordinances (Ezek. 36:26-27).

The parallel seems clear in 2 Corinthians. Paul declared that those who believed in Christ were living letters written on the heart by the Spirit of the living God. Their commitment did not come about as the result of letters chiseled in stone, but on tablets of the human heart (2 Cor. 3:3). It is the Spirit who gives life (2 Cor. 3:6). When a person accepts Christ, it is possible to read Moses as intended. "When one turns to the Lord, the veil is removed" (2 Cor. 3:16; see Exod. 34:34-35). So the new heart and new spirit arrive at the appearance of the Lord. "Now the Lord is the Spirit . . . for this comes from the Lord, the Spirit" (2 Cor. 3:17-18). Also in Galatians Paul apparently claims that the Spirit arrived to be present in the human heart at the coming of the Lord. "Well then, does God supply you with the Spirit and work miracles among you by your doing the works of the law, or by your believing what you heard?" (Gal. 3:5). The result is a new creation. "For neither circumcision nor uncircumcision is anything; but a new creation is everything!" (Gal. 6:15).

According to Paul the Spirit takes up his presence in those who respond to Christ at baptism. "For in the one Spirit we were all baptized into one body — Jews or Greeks, slaves or free — and we were all made to drink of one Spirit" (1 Cor. 12:13). Baptism corresponds to Christ's death, burial, and resurrection. "Therefore we have been buried with him by baptism into death, so that, just as Christ was raised from the dead by the glory of the Father, so we too might walk in newness of life" (Rom. 6:4). The new life is a Spirit-renewed and empowered life. "But you are not in the flesh; you are in the Spirit, since the Spirit of God dwells in you" (Rom. 8:9).

The chief feature of this new life in the Spirit is love. ". . . and hope does not disappoint us, because God's love has been poured into our hearts through the Holy Spirit that has been given us" (Rom. 5:5). In Galatians, Paul contrasted the works of the flesh to the fruit of the Spirit.

> Now the works of the flesh are obvious: fornication, impurity, licentiousness, idolatry, sorcery, enmities, strife, jealousy, anger, quarrels, dissensions, factions, envy, drunkenness, carousing, and things like these (Gal. 5:19-21).

The fruit of the Spirit is a completely different set of attributes. "By contrast, the fruit of the Spirit is love, joy, peace, patience, kindness, generosity, faithfulness, gentleness, and self-control. There is no law against such things" (Gal. 5:22-23). The believer is compelled by the love of Christ and the love which the Spirit pours into the heart (Rom. 5:5).

## The Gifts of the Spirit

If the Spirit chiefly pours love into the heart, and the first fruit of the Spirit is love, it is also the greatest of the gifts. "But strive for the greater gifts. And I will show you a still more excellent way" (1 Cor. 12:31). After extolling love, Paul concluded, "And now faith, hope, and love abide, these three; and the greatest of these is love" (1 Cor. 13:13).

There are, however, additional gifts the Spirit bestows upon those who believe. Paul anticipated that these would be multiple. Paul wrote the Romans, "For I am longing to see you so that I may share with you some spiritual gift to strengthen you — or rather so that we may be mutually encouraged by each other's faith, both yours and mine"

(Rom. 1:11-12). By this he did not imply that they had no spiritual gifts at all. Rather, he hoped to add to those they already possessed. Paul asserted that every believer was gifted by the Spirit of God. "But each has a particular gift from God, one having one kind and another a different kind" (1 Cor. 7:7). "We have gifts that differ according to the grace given to us" (Rom. 12:6; see also 1 Peter 4:10). Paul believed that at baptism members of the body are gifted by the Spirit for the body. Along the way, the Spirit may provide additional gifts, but no one is ungifted. It's like at Christmas time at our house. Everyone receives a gift. Through the years we have invited international students to enjoy the day with us. We made sure that these too received a gift. When God passes out the gifts, everyone receives at least one. Believers do not have to storm the walls of heaven so as to receive gifts. God gives them freely.

Believers then and now aspired to flashy gifts that impressed, especially at Corinth. Love is powerful, but it does not always impress. Paul, perhaps partly in irony, praised the Corinthians for possessing all the gifts. "[S]o that you are not lacking in any spiritual gift as you wait for the revealing of our Lord Jesus Christ" (1 Cor. 1:7).

But one can possess an abundance of gifts and still not be a loving, spiritual person. Consider that the Corinthians had every conceivable kind of gift, yet Paul accused them of being unspiritual. "And so, brothers and sisters, I could not speak to you as spiritual people, but rather as people of the flesh, as infants in Christ" (1 Cor. 3:1). They had, what to them were the flashy gifts, tongues and healing, but they did not get along with each other. "For as long as there is jealousy and quarreling among you, are you not of the flesh, and behaving according to human inclination?" (1 Cor. 3:3). They were quenching the greatest gift of all, that is, love.

Several years ago a group of students at Abilene Christian University became interested in the Neo-

Charismatic movement then sweeping the land. They participated in off-campus meetings in which people spoke in
tongues, prophesied, and sometimes claimed to heal the sick.
Administrators at the University became aware of these meetings, denounced the students for their participation, and
demanded that they no longer attend under the threat of
expulsion. Several of these students were in a class I taught.
One day a woman from among them came to my office. She
was agitated over the demands and very censorious in her
remarks about the administrators. I was shocked by the bitterness with which she spoke. Regardless of what one might
think about what the students were doing, or how the administrators were treating them, it struck me as odd that someone who prided herself in being filled by the Spirit of God
would utter these harsh and stinging words. I said to her,
"Paul says the Spirit pours love in our hearts. You claim to
have been overpowered by the Spirit of God. I am puzzled
therefore as to the source of the bitterness which seems to be
in your heart." She slowly recognized the discrepancy and
soon departed.

The Christians at Corinth had a special interest in the
spiritual gifts. They were boastful over these remarkable
skills. Paul saw the need to put the gifts in perspective at
some length in 1 Corinthians 12–14. "Now concerning the
spiritual gifts, brothers and sisters, I do not want you to be
uninformed" (1 Cor. 12:1). It seems that the chief gift of
interest at Corinth was speaking in tongues. It is only in
1 Corinthians that Paul mentioned this phenomenon even
though he lists *charismata* ("gifts") in other letters. The reason
Paul took up the matter only in this one letter may possibly
suggest that tongue speaking was singularly prevalent at
Corinth. The likelihood is that such speaking was popular
with certain cults in the city. With the conversion of persons
from these backgrounds, tongue speaking also cropped up in
the Christian assemblies. In 1 Corinthians 12:2, Paul charged

that some Corinthians were uncontrollably motivated in idol worship. "You know that when you were pagans, you were enticed and led astray to idols that could not speak." But now that they were filled with the Holy Spirit, they must be responsive to his control. Ecstatic outpourings can only come from him if they are consonant with his personhood. "Therefore I want you to understand that no one speaking by the Spirit of God ever says 'Let Jesus be cursed!' and no one can say 'Jesus is Lord' except by the Holy Spirit" (1 Cor. 12:3). If someone in the church, in an ecstatic high, cursed Jesus, then the ecstatic condition obviously was not the work of the Holy Spirit. Paul made it clear that not every gift claimed for the Spirit was of the Spirit.

Whether an alleged work of the Spirit was consistent with what is known about the Spirit was Paul's first test for assessing gifts as being exercised in Corinth. As he proceeded, he took up additional ways of determining whether gifts extolled by the Corinthians came from God.

The Greek word Paul employed consistently for "gifts" (1 Cor. 12–14) is *charisma*. The word in Greek means "gift," which has come into English as "charisma," meaning the personality of someone with a powerful influence on others, or "charismatic" which, at least, in religious circles means those who speak in tongues, prophesy, and heal. A "charismatic" gift, as conceived by charismatics, is therefore special, taking on a miraculous aura. Paul, however, did not distinguish gifts into two categories, that is, ordinary gifts and miraculous (charismatic) gifts. He did, however, rank the gifts as to importance, with love being the greatest of the gifts. In 1 Corinthians he devalued the gifts the Corinthians prized most, that is, tongue speaking and healing. All gifts, both ordinary, and, according to human thinking, "miraculous," Paul designated *charismata* indicating that he did not make the distinctions common both among modern charismatics and those who oppose them.

In Romans Paul listed the *charismata*,

> We have gifts [*charismata*] that differ according to the grace given to us: prophecy, in proportion to faith; ministry, in ministering; the teacher, in teaching; the exhorter, in exhortation; the giver, in generosity; the leader, in diligence; the compassionate, in cheerfulness (Rom. 12:6-8).

It would appear that these are not ranked according to importance. For example, the second gift is translated by the NIV "If it is serving, let him serve" (Rom. 12:7). This is a better translation in that "ministry" (NRSV) may imply being Minister of a church. Rather here the word means the more generic, "serving." The woman who heads the committee for education supplies, as well as the other members of the committee, serve the church. In Paul's language they have "charismatic gifts." The man who brings his favorite chili pie and mouth watering croissants to the potluck dinner serves the church. In Paul's designation he has a *charismata*, or as people in our time might say, a "charismatic gift."

In 1 Corinthians Paul taught that gifts (*charismata*) are of several varieties, but each have a common source, that is, God (1 Cor. 12:4-6). The gifts are not for personal aggrandizement, but for the collective good (1 Cor. 12:7). In this section the specific gifts (*charismata*) are: wisdom, utterance of knowledge, faith, healing, working of miracles, prophecy, discernment of spirits, and various kinds of tongues (1 Cor. 12:8-10). All these gifts are useful in the body and complement each other in their contribution to the common life of the church (1 Cor. 12:14-26). These gifts may also be considered from the perspective of the roles various people play in the church, that is, apostles, prophets, teachers, deeds of power, healing, forms of assistance, leadership, and various kinds of tongues (1 Cor. 12:28-30). No one person, Paul declared, fulfilled all these roles or possessed all these gifts. It would seem in this case (1 Cor. 12:28-30) that Paul ranked the roles or gifts according to their importance, as he understood it. The gift of least importance therefore, as he viewed it, was speaking in various kinds of tongues. But the most important gift was love.

In chapter thirteen of 1 Corinthians, Paul heralded the ultimate importance of love for the church. Persons in Corinth or elsewhere, might speak Greek, Latin, or Celtic, and some may even speak a special language identified as "angelic" (1 Cor. 13:1). They may also possess great prophetic powers and be able to explain mysterious and complex concepts. Their faith may be impeccable — so great that they can move mountains. They may have such disdain for what they have that they give it all away or even their own bodies. But if they don't have the gift (*charismata*) of love, it is of no consequence (1 Cor. 13:1-3). The church can press ahead without prophecy or special knowledge (1 Cor. 13:10), and while it may still prevail without love, it will not be the church of the God whose very being is love. The mark of the perfect or mature church is love. "When the complete (*teleios*, KJV "perfect") comes, the partial will come to an end" (1 Cor. 13:10). At the end of the nineteenth century some declared that the coming of the perfect was the completion of the New Testament. But in this context *teleios* obviously means either maturing in love (see 1 Cor. 2:6 where *teleios* is commonly translated mature though the KJV has "perfect") or the return of Christ (1 Cor. 13:12), or both. Paul therefore declared that whatever the value of prophecy or tongues to the church, the ultimate gift is love.

A second criterion, therefore, for evaluating the gifts, the first being consistency with what is known to be the work of the Holy Spirit, is whether gifts (*charismata*) promote love. If gifts destroy a common concern of persons in the body for each other, then the church is better off without them. In 1 Corinthians 14 Paul charged that tongues as practiced at Corinth resulted in confusion rather than upbuilding, encouragement, and consolation (1 Cor. 14:3), thereby offering a third criterion. The Greek word translated "upbuilding" (NRSV) *oikodomeo* is translated "edify" in older versions. Gifts, and here Paul focused on the gifts of tongues, must build up the church, not disrupt it.

I think that in 1 Corinthians 14 Paul had in mind various sorts of tongues, for example, Greek, Latin, and Phoenician, but also a special "angelic tongue" which no one recognized as a human language. Apparently it was the latter in which the Corinthians were the most interested. Paul described this "angelic tongue" as one which no one understood (1 Cor. 14:2) except for God. The "angelic tongue" may build up the person uttering it, but it does not build up the church (1 Cor. 14:4). The only way in which it can build up the church, Paul declared, was for someone to interpret the utterance (1 Cor. 14:5,13). It is not clear to me whether Paul also professed to speak in this "angelic" language (1 Cor. 14:17), but I do think that when he wrote, "I thank God that I speak in tongues more than all of you" (1 Cor. 14:18) that he had in mind the many human languages he spoke, the "varieties of tongues," as he called them, as well as perhaps the "angelic tongue." The "angelic tongue" as practiced in Corinth was therefore different from the tongues of Acts 2, or "other languages" (Acts 2:4). At Jerusalem, as believers spoke, "each one heard them speaking in the native language of each" (Acts 2:6).

Members of the church may speak in different tongues and this may at first attract unbelievers, but it will be of no benefit to them (1 Cor. 14:20-25). It is only when they make sense of what is being said from one source that they will be convicted. So Paul concluded, "I would rather speak five words with my mind, in order to instruct others also, than ten thousand words in a tongue" (1 Cor. 14:18-19).

Whatever happens in the church should build up the church, both the believers and visitors alike. What was happening in the Corinthian church was not achieving that end.

In the first place, utterances were arising from various quarters in the assembly which no one understood. And to compound the confusion, several were speaking at once. Paul charged that confusion of this sort did not come from the Holy Spirit of God, regardless of what the Corinthians claimed, ". . . for God is a God not of disorder but of peace" (1 Cor. 14:33). When God gives utterance to the prophets, the prophets can bring their message to the congregation in an orderly fashion (1 Cor. 14:32). "If a revelation is made to someone else sitting nearby, let the first person be silent" (1 Cor. 14:30). So the contribution of "angelic tongues" to the church is minimal, and even may be detrimental if uncontrolled.

The Holy Spirit of God empowers the church so that Christ's earthly ministry continues until his return. The Holy Spirit dwells in the church (1 Cor. 3:16) and in the individual believer, producing the fruit of the Spirit. The Spirit showers the church with faith, hope, and love. The Holy Spirit gifts the body for the common good so that God may be glorified on earth.

# Questions for Discussion

1. Are the disciples of Christ baptized with the Holy Spirit, then and now?

2. Were the disciples of Jesus Spirit-filled during the time of Jesus' ministry?

3. What is the best translation of *parakletos* (John 14)?

4. What, according to the Gospel of John, will the Holy Spirit accomplish?

5. What is the test for those who claim special knowledge from God (1 John)?

6. What is special about the fall of the Spirit in Acts 2 and Acts 10?

7. What is the gift of the Spirit (Acts 2:39)?

8. According to Paul, what are the characteristics of a Spirit-filled person?

9. How and when do disciples receive the gifts of the Spirit according to Paul?

10. How does Paul think gifts claimed for the Spirit are to be tested?

11. As Paul employed the word *charismata*, do all believers have a charismatic gift?

12. Did Paul think that tongues, as practiced at Corinth, were from God?

# 11
# He Called the Church into Being

$\mathcal{T}$he outcome of the earthly ministry of Jesus was the dotting of committed groups of believers across the Mediterranean landscape. Much more is written about the church in the epistles than in the Gospels. But many statements of Jesus in the Gospels lead us to conclude that Jesus anticipated the planting of communities of faith.

## *The Church in the Gospels*

The Greek word, normally translated "church" (*ekklesia*), occurs three times in the four Gospels and all three are in the Gospel of Matthew (16:18 and twice in 18:17). But anticipation of the church may be found in other ways, for example, in connection with the kingdom of God or in Matthew, the kingdom of heaven. In regard to the Synoptics, I will focus on Matthew since this Gospel has more observations on the church than either Mark or Luke. I will first notice how Matthew positions the church in his overall structure, then comment on the church in the sayings of Jesus.

## Have Seen a Great Light

Early in Matthew it is clear that Jesus is God's new king, not just for Israel, but for the world. The powers that be in Palestine may ignore him or try to kill him, but potentates from distant Eastern lands pay their respects, bearing gifts (Matt. 2:1-12). The devil offered Jesus the kingdoms of the world under his auspices, but Jesus refused, opting rather for a role in the universal spread of God's kingdom (Matt. 4:8-10). Matthew next reported the arrest of John the Baptist and the inception of Jesus' ministry. Matthew provides a motif for Jesus' ministry by citing Isaiah 9:1-2.

> "Land of Zebulun, land of Naphtali,
> on the road by the sea, across the Jordan, Galilee of the Gentiles —
> the people who sat in darkness
> have seen a great light (Matt. 4:15-16).

This statement has far more significance to the Gospel of Matthew than may at first be apparent. From the region of Galilee of the Gentiles a light radiates which will eventually spread throughout the world.

Matthew is fascinated by the manner in which the kingdom of heaven, initiated by the ministry of Jesus in Palestine, will radiate throughout the world as a great light overcoming darkness. Those in the kingdom of heaven are to let their light shine.

> "You are the light of the world. A city built on a hill cannot be hid.
> In the same way, let your light shine before others, so that they may
> see your good works and give glory to your Father in heaven" (Matt.
> 5:14,16).

The citizens of the kingdom are to overcome darkness and internalize light (Matt. 6:22-23). All aspects of existence will eventually be exposed to light and the message of Jesus is to be proclaimed from the housetops (Matt. 10:26-28). At the end the sun, moon and stars will be darkened and then the Son of Man will appear from heaven in power and glory (Matt. 24:28-31). The angels will gather from one end of heaven to another those who have been a light to the world.

The spread of the kingdom by its light reminds one of the candle demonstration. All the persons in a room are given a candle. They are told that the candles will be lighted one at a time from the flame of a first candle. The lights are turned off. The first candle is lighted. A glimmer of light shines in the darkness. Now a second candle is lighted from the first. The room becomes brighter. Now candle after candle is lighted from one nearby. Finally, with all the candles aflame, the darkness has been pushed aside and the faces of all in the room are clearly visible. In this manner the kingdom of God overcomes the darkness of the world! "Go therefore and make disciples of all nations" (Matt. 28:18; see also 24:14).

The story of Jesus, his teaching and ways, have enlightened his disciples. They are to now go beyond the borders of Israel into all the world. The kingdom of heaven is like yeast which spreads throughout the dough until all is eventually leavened (Matt. 13:33).

## Jesus on the Kingdom

Central to the proclamation of Jesus was "Repent, for the kingdom of heaven has come near" (Matt. 4:17). That was also the message of John the Baptist (Matt. 3:2) and the word Jesus charged his disciples to proclaim in the cities of Israel (Matt. 10:7). What is this kingdom and is it the same as the church?

In the Sermon on the Mount Jesus offered his observations on the characteristics of those who would be a part of the kingdom. "Blessed are the poor in spirit, for theirs is the kingdom of heaven" (Matt. 5:3; also 5:10,19; 6:10,33). Obviously the kingdom is to be a concrete entity of people on earth (Matt. 6:33). Some will enter the kingdom, and some, though thinking they are in the kingdom, will discover, to their dismay, that they are not (Matt. 7:21). The kingdom of heaven will be unlike the kingdoms of men where power and prestige prevail. It will be a kingdom in which servanthood reigns (Matt. 20:24-28). These characteristics are developed more fully in chapter 6 on the teaching of Jesus.

In a series of parables Jesus made it clear that the kingdom of God will expand throughout the earth. It will be like the substantial plant which grows from a small mustard seed (Matt. 13:31-32). But many people will resist.

**"The angels will come out and separate the evil from the righteous and throw them into the furnace of fire, where there will be weeping and gnashing of teeth" (Matt. 13:49-50).**

Many in Israel who presume they are God's people will turn down the invitation to enter the kingdom and will be rejected (Matt. 21:43–22:14).

In a sense the kingdom had already arrived upon earth because God was present in Jesus. Wherever God's rule and power prevails, there also is the kingdom of God. When the Pharisees, put off by the way in which others idolized Jesus, charged that his power came from Beelzebul, the ruler of demons, Jesus replied, "But if it is by the Spirit of God that I cast out demons, then the kingdom of God has come to you" (Matt. 12:28). Though the kingdom of God was present in Jesus on earth, it also transcended earth, that is, the kingdom of God exists where God is. Those who become a part of the kingdom on earth will upon death sit down with those already in the kingdom in heaven. "I tell you, many will come from east and west and will eat with Abraham and Isaac and Jacob in the kingdom of heaven" (Matt. 8:11). The faithful will "inherit the kingdom prepared for you from the foundation of the world" (Matt. 25:34).

There is a sense, however, in which the church and the kingdom are one and the same on earth. Jesus used the two terms interchangeably.

"And I tell you, you are Peter, and on this rock I will build my church, and the gates of Hades will not prevail against it. I will give you the keys of the kingdom of heaven, and whatever you bind on earth will be bound in heaven, and whatever you loose on earth will be loosed in heaven" (Matt. 16:18-19).

The declaration that what the disciples decided on earth would also obtain in heaven is found again in regard to offenses and disputes in the church (Matt. 18:15-19). The kingdom and the church are one and the same in that wherever the church has gathered, there is a concrete location of the kingdom of heaven upon earth. However, the kingdom of heaven is not limited to the earthly church. The kingdom of God existed before the church came into being and will continue to exist when earth and the church are no more. When one reads the word "church" in Scripture one can also assume the word refers to the earthly manifestation of the kingdom of God. But when one reads the phrase, "kingdom of God" in the Scripture one may not presume that the reference is always to the church.

### I Am the Vine

Jesus envisioned that the disciples would carry on his earthly ministry despite his death. His ministry would continue because he was ascending "to my Father and your Father, to my God and your God" (John 20:17). As a replacement, he would send the Divine Helper to be with them forever (John 14:16; 20:22). The kingdom of God is mentioned three times in John, first in John 3:5, in which Jesus told Nicodemus that he must be born of the water and of the Spirit in order to enter the kingdom of God, and twice in John 18:36 in responding to Pilate's question as to whether he was king of the Jews. Jesus declared, "My kingdom is not from this world. If my kingdom were from this world, my followers would be fighting . . ." (John 18:36). It is not certain in either case that Jesus was speaking of the church though it seems that one who is born from above commences involvement in the kingdom here and now, or in other words in the church.

Jesus employed two "I am" metaphors which clearly refer to the church. "I am the good shepherd" (John 10:14) and "I am the vine" (John 15:5). That Jesus is the good shepherd implied that he has a flock. He is the leader of the flock. He will lay down his life for the sheep (John 10:11). He knows which sheep are his (John 10:14). He has other sheep not now in his fold which are to be added (John 10:16). These are the Gentiles who will enter along with the Jewish believers, so that there will be one flock and one shepherd. We can label this a *sociological metaphor* in which followers are dependent upon a leader. The church of Jesus Christ is cared for and protected by its true shepherd.

In the second metaphor Christ is the vine and the father is the vinegrower. Those who accept Jesus as Lord and Savior are the branches (John 15:1,5). God is therefore the owner of the vineyard. Jesus is the vine that nurtures the branches. The disciples, that is the branches, receive their growing power and sustenance from Jesus, the vine. If they abide in the vine they will bear fruit (John 15:5). Whatever the branches require will be provided (John 15:7). In this case the metaphor is a *botanical* one. Just as the vine gives nutrients to the branches, so Jesus empowers the church. In the Gospel of John therefore, the church is that flock which thrives because of its loving shepherd, and the branches that produce fruit as the result of life-sustaining ingredients provided by the vine.

## *At the Right Hand of God*

In Luke-Acts the church is comprised of those groups which sprang up all the way to the ends of the earth, and is therefore the concretized kingdom of God upon earth. During the forty days after his resurrection, before he was taken up, Jesus spoke about the kingdom of God (Acts 1:3). As the departure approached, the disciples asked, "Lord, is this the time when you will restore the kingdom to Israel?" (Acts 1:6). Jesus responded that it was not for them to know the time. But he promised that they would receive "power when the Holy Spirit has come upon you" (Acts 1:7-8). When Jesus was taken up, the disciples looked skyward. Soon two men asked, "Why do you stand here looking up toward heaven? This Jesus, who has been taken up from you into heaven, will come in the same way as you saw him go into heaven" (Acts 1:11). The intention of Jesus seems to be that the kingdom has indeed commenced under the auspices of the Holy Spirit. "And see, I am sending upon you what my Father promised" (Luke 24:49). From God's side the exalted Jesus poured out that Holy Spirit (Acts 2:33). Also at that right hand Jesus stood so as to sustain the church as it continued his earthly ministry. According to Stephen, Jesus witnessed the events leading to his death. "I see the heavens opened and the Son of Man standing at the right hand of God!"(Acts 7:56).

The church grew by leaps and bounds, first by the 3,000 who responded to Peter's command, "Repent, and be baptized every one of you in the name of Jesus Christ so that your sins may be forgiven; and you will receive the gift of the Holy Spirit" (Acts 2:38). God added them to the church (Acts 2:47). Later five thousand accepted Christ as Lord (Acts 4:4). These early believers shared fellowship, teaching, possessions, and food (Acts 2:41-47). The church appointed men to care for the widows (6:1-6). After the church was persecuted, the leaders traveled throughout the region planting congregations (8:1-3). A church was planted in Antioch consisting of both Jews and Gentiles (Acts 11:19-26), and as a result of its strategic position and ethnic diversity additional churches were established throughout Asia Minor and Greece (Acts 13). The church in Jerusalem, upon a decision by the apostles and elders, accepted the mission of Paul to the Gentiles (Acts 15). As the church spread, elders and deacons were appointed to lead and teach. "Keep watch over yourselves and all the flock, of which the Holy Spirit has made you overseers, to shepherd the church of God that he obtained with the blood of his own Son" (Acts 20:28). The church is the embodiment of the resurrected Christ in communities of faith crisscrossing the Mediterranean region.

## The Church in the Epistles

### Because of the Body on the Cross

Paul chiefly depicted the church through employing the metaphor of a human body. We might label this an *anthropological model*, as contrasted with the vine in John, that is, the *botanical model*.

> For as in one body we have many members, and not all the members have the same function, so we, who are many, are one body in Christ, and individually we are members one of another (Rom. 12:4-5).

The different functions of persons in the body, that is, the church, are supplied by the Holy Spirit. "We have gifts that differ according to the grace given to us" (Rom. 12:6; see also 1 Cor. 12:12-27).

The body, the church, came about as the result of the proclamation of "the gospel concerning his Son, who was descended from David according to the flesh and was declared to be Son of God with power according to the Spirit of holiness by resurrection from the dead, Jesus Christ our Lord" (Rom. 1:3-4). It was because of Christ's body on the cross that this body, the church, came into being. "But God proves his love for us in that while we still were sinners Christ died for us" (Rom. 5:8). When the Lord's supper is observed, both the body on the cross and the body of believers should be in mind. "Whoever, therefore, eats the bread or drinks the cup of the Lord in an unworthy manner will be answerable for the body and blood of the Lord" (1 Cor. 11:27).

Paul charged the Corinthians, "Examine yourselves, and only then eat of the bread and drink of the cup" (1 Cor. 11:28). What does this mean? Does the person who best imagines the extreme suffering of the Son on the cross please God the most? Paul went on to write, "For all who eat and drink without discerning the body, eat and drink judgment against themselves" (1 Cor. 11:29). The problem at Corinth was that those of affluence who came early did not wait to share their bounty with late arrivals who had little. The body therefore that they did not discern, was not only the body on the cross, but the body brought into being by Christ's body. Members of the church should "have the same care for one another. If one member suffers, all suffer together with it; if one member is honored, all rejoice together with it" (1 Cor. 12:25-26). Discerning the body in the situation at Corinth therefore implies that the members wait for one another when they eat the Lord's Supper (1 Cor. 11:33). It may have little to do with a vivid sense of the gravity of Christ's death. The church is a body of persons who love each other because Christ, in his body on the cross, demonstrated his preeminent love for them.

In another metaphor Paul compared the church with a temple of worshipers — a sanctified assembly analogy. Such an assembly is empowered by God through the Holy Spirit. The believers in Corinth were filled with jealousy, quarreling and divided in various ways. Paul warned them that they were in danger of being rejected by God.

> Do you not know that you are God's temple and that God's Spirit dwells in you? If anyone destroys God's temple, God will destroy that person. For God's temple is holy, and you are that temple (1 Cor. 3:16-17).

The church is not God's church through its own drive and aspirations. It is God's church because the Holy Spirit dwells within the body corporately and energizes it. But Paul can, of course, also write of the Spirit indwelling individually in the believer (1 Cor. 6:19).

### Before the Foundation of the World

In the advent of his Son upon the earth God brought to fruition his plans of long standing to reconcile humans to himself and to each other.

[A]ccording to his good pleasure that he set forth in Christ, as a plan for the fullness of time, to gather up all things in him, things in heaven and things on earth (Eph. 1:9-10).

Through the death and resurrection of Christ, God has made one with himself those who are his, and in turn each believer with another. The church is that body at one with all the powers in heaven and with all those on earth who name Christ as Lord. "And he has put all things under his feet and has made him the head over all things for the church, which is his body, the fullness of him who fills all in all" (Eph. 1:22). Christ through his obedient death has been assigned headship over all that is. Christ is therefore the head of the church which is his body. The church extends from heaven, where its head is located, to the earth, where the body is situated. Though on earth, the church is also situated with its head in the heavenly places, ". . . and raised us up with him and seated us with him in the heavenly places in Christ Jesus" (Eph. 2:6).

The metaphor of headship in Ephesians, though at first political, that is, Christ is head of the realm of God which extends from heaven to the earth, later draws upon the marriage analogy. "For the husband is the head of the wife just as Christ is the head of the church, the body of which he is the Savior" (Eph. 5:23). Christ as head supplies the body with a model of servanthood. "Christ loved the church and gave himself up for her" (Eph. 5:25). Therefore the church as the bride of Christ gives itself up to Christ as head, and the members to each other, just as Christ gave himself up for the church. "Be subject to one another out of reverence for Christ" (Eph. 5:21).

Because Christ gave himself up for the church he made it holy and without blemish, not so much in its features, but in its very life.

> Christ loved the church and gave himself up for her, in order to make her holy by cleansing her with the washing of water by the word, so as to present the church to himself in splendor, without a spot or wrinkle or anything of the kind — yes, so that she may be holy and without blemish (Eph. 5:25-27).

The church is holy because Christ himself has removed all the sin and stain from the church. "In him we have redemption through his blood, the forgiveness of our trespasses, according to the riches of his grace that he lavished on us" (Eph. 1:7-8). Ephesians 5:25-27 from at least the time of the Puritans on has been employed to charge the committed with ridding the church of human inventions. And it has indeed been the case that encrustations sometimes need removal so as to get back to the basics. But the declaration of this text is that Christ has purified the church from the sin within the believers, and not from the defilement of its overt structures.

## We Have Fellowship with One Another

A theology of the church is especially robust in 1 John. The focus on the church came about as the result of a challenge to the faithful by some who left (1 John 2:8). Because of the manner in which John set out to reassure those who remained, it appears that those who left claimed an untouchable God (1:1-3), special knowledge (2:3,13,21,2 ), sinlessness (1:8–2:2; 3:4-10; 5:16-19), a special anointing (2:20,27; 3:24–4:6,15), a walk in the light (1:7; 2:9), immediate eternal life (5:13); and that it was imperative that they leave

these run-of-the-mill believers in order to pursue higher spir-
ituality (2:15; 4:19–5:5). These quitters considered themselves spiritually superior.

John, in his response, disputed their claims, asserting
that those who remained were, in fact, grounded in the true
faith. In the first place, God himself in Christ entered into an
intimate relationship with humans. God did not break off
relations with those inferior to himself but entered into a
common life with them. Those who left envisioned God
incorrectly, and as a result, related to their fellows inappro-
priately. The God who was from the beginning did not with-
hold himself. The first believers saw, touched, and heard the
one who entered into their midst. They, at his instigation,
entered into fellowship with "the Father and with his Son
Jesus Christ" (1 John 1:3). These believers, in turn, reported
this experience to those who populated the churches. Because
God had entered into an intimate relationship with the first
believers, they in turn shared life with others at some distance from where the original rapprochement occurred.

So convinced were those who left that God distanced
himself from what is earthy and human, they rejected the
fundamental claim of John that God himself came in the
flesh (1 John 4:2). They refused to consent to John's claim
that Jesus "has been born of God" (1 John 5:1). They apparently believed that "the Christ" inhabited the man Jesus, but
was not identical with him. Their views were likely similar to
those of Cerinthus, who flourished late in the first century,
who asserted that "the Christ" entered the man Jesus at his
baptism but departed for heaven before Jesus died on the
cross. Because God refused to fellowship with inferior matter
and sinful humans, those who abandoned the churches felt
justified in rejecting and leaving behind their inferior fellows.
Their erroneous doctrine of God resulted in a fallacious doctrine of the church.

God was not one to hold himself at arm's length from humankind. He sent his very Son to be born of woman, to become fully human in the flesh. The Greek word translated "fellowship" is *koinonia*. It means to enter into communion or partnership with another. God is himself *koinonia*, that is, he reached out first. "We love because he first loved us" (1 John 4:19). John also declared that God is light (1 John 1:5). What can it mean that God is light, other than that he steadfastly enters into the life of humankind? The person who is in the light, like God, loves his brothers and sisters (1 John 2:10). The person, contrariwise, who hates a brother or sister is in darkness (1 John 2:9). Therefore to "walk in the light as he himself is in the light . . ." (1 John 1:7) implies being Godlike through *koinonia*, that is, fellowship. To walk in the light of God is not specifically to hold a series of doctrines in common with others, however desirable that may be, but to exhibit a loving life in the Lord. Those who left had it all wrong. Rather than cutting out from the inferior believers, they should have stayed and lifted them up just as God did in Christ. "We know love by this, that he laid down his life for us — and we ought to lay down our lives for one another" (1 John 3:16).

The church of Jesus Christ has been called into being by a God who seeks out humans for fellowship. They in turn seek to share life with others. Because of their love for each other they comprise a church in which sin is being forgiven. "If we walk in the light as he himself is in the light, we have fellowship with one another, and the blood of Jesus his Son cleanses us from all sin" (1 John 1:7). Those who leave the body of faith, therefore situate themselves outside the context in which sin is being forgiven. Since God is himself fellowship, he will not forgive the sins of those who reject fellowship.

I think therefore that, in the context of 1 John, the mortal sin, or the sin unto death, is to drop out of the church. John wrote:

> If you see your brother or sister committing what is not a mortal sin, you will ask, and God will give life to such a one — to those whose sin is not mortal. There is sin that is mortal; I do not say that you should pray about that. All wrongdoing is sin, but there is sin that is not mortal (1 John 5:16-17).

The believer should not pray that the one who has left the fellowship be forgiven for having left. Those who departed denied the basic being of God. God forgives those who remain in fellowship. The ones left behind, no doubt, committed many sins. By their faithfulness, if they do sin, they "have an advocate with the Father, Jesus Christ the righteous" (1 John 2:1). The church therefore possesses an enviable privilege. By its prayers, sins are forgiven for those who flourish within its confines.

## Servanthood Leadership

Leadership in the church emulates its Lord. "For the Son of Man came not to be served but to serve, and to give his life a ransom for many" (Mark 10:45). The leaders of the church just like the first Shepherd of the church are willing to lay down their life for the sheep (John 10:15). They are to be examples to the flock through serving.

> Do not lord it over those in your charge, but be examples to the flock. And when the chief shepherd appears, you will win the crown of glory that never fades away (1 Peter 5:3-4).

The shepherd does not bestow upon the sheep the facility for changing grass into wool and lamb. Sheep are productive because God has gifted them with the talent of producing meat and wool. A good shepherd is the one who sees to it that a safe and fruitful environment is available so that the sheep can profitably utilize the gifts God supplies. So it is in the church. The Holy Spirit has gifted the church with many talents, each of which contribute to the common good. The shepherds of the flock, that is, the elders, do not determine how the flock is gifted, nor are they to decide which gifts may be employed in the flock and which ones not. If God supplied the gifts, he intended that they be employed for the body. The leaders of the church have special gifts, that is, gifts of teaching and administration. They see to it that the church provides an environment in which each member may exercise her or his gifts. They lead the sheep into favorable pastures where water is available. They see to it that predators do not harass the flock.

Woe to those leaders who take it upon themselves to squash the gifts God has supplied to the members of his church!

The effective leaders among God's people are full of faith, wisdom, and the Holy Spirit (Acts 6:3-5). They are worthy persons, above reproach. They are committed to their spouses (1 Tim. 3:2). They must be capable managers of their households as an indication that they can capably manage the household of God (1 Tim. 3:5). The elders as well as the deacons must be serious, straight speaking, not overindulgent in wine, nor greedy, and temperate (1 Tim. 3:8-13). They must love the church as did Christ and treat her as a beloved bride.

## *Baptism*

Entry into the kingdom of God, and therefore to the church, is, according to Jesus, through one baptism — the baptism of water and the Spirit (John 3:5). John the Baptist baptized in water (John 1:26) as did Jesus' disciples (John 4:2). Some recently have argued that the water (3:5) is the water of the embryo sack. However, the Greek mitigates against this as does Nicodemus's discussion with Jesus. Neither Nicodemus nor Jesus is interested in discussing biological birth. It is assumed. The question is: how is one born from above or again? Jesus declared that the new birth is the result of being "born of water and Spirit." Paul made the same point. "For in the one Spirit we were all baptized into one body — Jews or Greeks, slaves or free — and we were all made to drink of one Spirit" (1 Cor. 12:13). It is clear from Paul's analogy of baptism with the death, burial, and resurrection of Christ, that he had in mind by analogy, going down into the water, that is, immersion, and the coming up out of the water (Rom. 6:3-4). Paul declared that there is one baptism (Eph. 4:5). That one baptism is baptism of the water and the Spirit.

Baptism may be said to be an outward sign of an inward grace. By being immersed in water the believer indicates an acceptance of God's gift of forgiveness of sins through the death of Jesus Christ. Ananias, after the Lord had appeared to Paul on the way to Damascus, declared to him, "And now why do you delay? Get up, be baptized, and have your sins washed away, calling on his name" (Acts 22:16). At that same time Paul received the Holy Spirit (Acts 9:17-19). Baptism may be said to save those who submit to it in that through baptism the believer expresses a confidence in the saving power of God in the resurrection of Jesus Christ. "And baptism, which this prefigured, now saves you — not as a removal of dirt from the body, but as an appeal to God for a good conscience, through the resurrection of Jesus Christ" (1 Pet. 3:21). Believers are saved by the death and resurrection of Jesus Christ. Baptism is the sign that they have received this marvelous gift from God. Peter did not by his declaration affirm baptismal regeneration, that is, that baptism itself conferred the new life. Regeneration happened, not because of the baptism, but because of the power of God in the resurrection of Jesus Christ. Salvation is made possible by God and him alone. "For God so loved the world that he gave his only Son, so that everyone who believes in him may not perish but may have eternal life" (John 3:16). The one who receives this salvation reaches out to lay hold to it and thereby expresses a confidence in the action of God. "Because if you confess with your lips that Jesus is Lord and believe in your heart that God raised him from the dead, you will be saved. For one believes with the heart and so is justified, and one confesses with the mouth and so is saved" (Rom. 10:9-10).

A preacher I once heard in Pennsylvania employed as the title of his sermon, "Salvation equals God's Part + Man's Part." Very little was said about God's part. The majority of the time was spent on man's part. Man's part, he explained, is to hear, believe, repent, confess, and be baptized. Of these five, he stressed baptism the most. In the writings of Paul much more is said about God's part, that is, what God has done to reconcile humankind to himself.

In the middle 1960's the Hershey Foundation of Hershey, Pennsylvania, gave The Pennsylvania State University fifty million dollars to build a medical school in Derry Township. The money from the Foundation had to be spent in that Township. The newspaper account included a picture of Eric Walker, President of Penn State, receiving a check from the President of the foundation. The article gave no details about Eric Walker, and little about Penn State. The article was about Milton S. Hershey (1857-1945) founder of the Hershey Chocolate Company. Hershey was unmarried and without family. While alive he used many of his resources to improve the quality of life in Derry Township and his Foundation was instructed, upon his death, to spend all its assets there. The article presumed that Eric Walker's part was simply to receive the check presented. Of course, Penn State committed itself to build the Medical School.

The announcement of salvation should likewise focus upon God's part. The emphasis on what humans do distorts the true situation. The announcement about salvation should highlight God's great gift. Emphasis upon either the faith or baptism of the recipient misconstrues the salvific action of God in Christ (Rom. 6:3-4).

## When I Drink It New in the Kingdom of God

The entry into the body of Christ is by gladly accepting the magnificent gift from God and being buried with Christ in baptism. In the body, the church, believers regularly feast with the risen Lord.

> He said to them, "This is my blood of the covenant, which is poured out for many. Truly I tell you, I will never again drink of the fruit of the vine until that day when I drink it new in the kingdom of God" (Mark 14:24-25).

As believers eat the Supper with the Lord and with each other, they are reminded that he gave his body and his blood on their behalf. The focus is not on the eating, but what the host, who has invited believers to the table, has done on their behalf. Those who participate too, no doubt, are to be reminded that whenever Jesus gives a feast, no one goes away hungry. Baskets of leftovers are taken up (Mark 6:42-43; 8:8). Whenever the Lord's supper is eaten, the Lord's body is nourished. The Lord's Supper likewise is an outward show of inner grace. The grace of God in the death of his Son was concretized upon the earth. Now Jesus is seated at the right hand of God. When believers on earth eat, he is present. In feasting with Jesus at his table, representatives from both heaven and earth are present. Something occurs both in heaven and upon earth.

The church of Jesus Christ is the continuing ministry on earth of the resurrected Lord. The church is his body. It is the body brought about because of his body on the cross. It is the sanctified temple, empowered by the Holy Spirit of God. Within its walls are salvation and forgiveness of sins.

# Questions for Discussion

1. How many times and where is the word church used in the four Gospels?

2. Did Jesus intend to found churches?

3. Was the kingdom of God present on earth during the earthly ministry of Jesus?

4. Every time the phrase "kingdom of God" is employed, is it appropriate to substitute the word church?

5. By what analogies does Jesus discuss the church in John?

6. How does Acts contribute to a theology of the church?

7. What is Paul's chief metaphor for the church?

8. What does Paul mean when he declares that those who participate in the Lord's Supper must discern the body?

9. How does one walk in the light as God is in the light?

10. How does one become a member of the church?

11. What are the chief responsibilities of elders of the church?

12. How does the Lord's Supper proclaim the gospel until he comes?

# 12
# He Showed No Partiality

*I*n the New Testament, the death and resurrection of Christ not only reconciled humans to God, but to one another. Contrariwise, in Genesis, humans, through their desire to be like the gods, became estranged from the Lord God (Gen. 3) and from each other (Gen. 11). Because they set out to make a name for themselves "the LORD confused the language of all the earth; and from there the LORD scattered them abroad over the face of all the earth" (Gen. 11:9).

On the feast of Pentecost, persons from many nations made a pilgrimage to Jerusalem. To their wonderment, as the disciples of Christ spoke, despite the many languages of those present, the age old barriers dropped away. "Amazed and astonished, they asked, 'Are not all these who are speaking Galileans? And how is it that we hear, each of us, in our own native language?'" (Acts 2:7-8). Christ not only overcame the separation of humans from God, but also from each other. Those present on this memorable feast day later heard the disciples declare that because of Christ, God would forgive their sins. By Christ's actions they could attain a new relationship with God. The disciples were commissioned to spread this astonishing news to all nations and peoples, even to the ends of the earth.

As Peter spoke to the Gentiles gathered at Cornelius's house in Caesarea, he declared with new found conviction that because of Jesus Christ, ancient walls were removed.

> **"I truly understand that God shows no partiality, but in every nation anyone who fears him and does what is right is acceptable to him. You know the message he sent to the people of Israel, preaching peace by Jesus Christ — he is Lord of all" (Acts 10:34-36).**

Each of the Gospels in their own way declared, often in the parables, that Jesus came not only as Savior of Israel but also of all humankind. We have already noticed in Matthew that the advent of Jesus created light in Galilee of the Gentiles.

## Welcome One Another, Therefore, Just as Christ Has Welcomed You

Many of the strains and stresses among the early believers were because of ethnic differences. Chief among these were the Jewish disdain for uncircumcised Gentiles and the Gentile perception of Jews as a nonconforming minority. But in addition, there were class and economic biases. Paul anticipated that because of the action of Christ, and despite their differences, believers would work, love, and care for each other. "There is no longer Jew or Greek, there is no longer slave or free, there is no longer male and female; for all of you are one in Christ Jesus" (Gal. 3:28). Of course, Paul did not believe that because of Christ gender differences would disappear, or that anytime soon there would no longer be slaves or Jews. What he desired more than anything else was the ability of the persons of diverse stations in life to work together lovingly in spite of their differences.

Paul addressed these matters as they related to the situation in Rome. In the first place believers should not parade their own personal worth. "For by the grace given to me I say to everyone among you not to think of yourself more highly than you ought to think, but to think with sober judgment, each according to the measure of faith that God has assigned" (Rom. 12:3). God has gifted each person for the benefit of the body and these varying gifts should be accepted and recognized. Christians should "love one another with mutual affection; outdo one another in showing honor" (Rom. 12:10). Furthermore, they should "Live in harmony with one another; do not be haughty, but associate with the lowly; do not claim to be wiser than you are" (Rom. 12:16). And, "If it is possible, so far as it depends on you, live peaceably with all" (Rom. 12:18).

In chapter 14 of Romans Paul addressed more specifically the situation as he understood it in the churches in Rome. Christianity commenced in Rome rather early, perhaps when converts returned from Jerusalem after the feast of Pentecost (Acts 2:10). During the next several years house churches sprang up in the city among the some forty thousand Jews living there, as well as among local Romans and immigrants. Because of disturbances in the Jewish community in the late 40s A.D., Jews were banned from Rome and this included Jews who converted to Christianity. Among these were Aquila and Priscilla "who had recently come from Italy . . . because Claudius had ordered all Jews to leave Rome" (Acts 18:2). About this ban, Suetonius, a Roman author in his *Life of Claudius*, wrote in A.D. 49, "Since the Jews constantly make disturbances at the instigation of Chrestus, he expelled them from Rome." Upon the departure of the Jews, both those who had embraced Jesus as Messiah and those who hadn't, Christianity continued to grow among the Roman Gentiles. In A.D. 54, five years later, Claudius died and Nero came to the throne. Nero's wife was favorable toward the Jews, according to Josephus, and perhaps she was even a convert. So the Jews were permitted to return to Rome.

The Jewish Christians in Rome now faced a new situation. When they were forced out of Rome, they were likely in the majority, but now they were a returning minority. Romans 16 indicates several house churches, and by the names there probably were at least five which may be identified: (1) a Jewish group, 16:3-7; (2) a Roman, Latin-speaking group. 16:10; (3) a Greek-speaking group, 16:11; (4) a second Latin-speaking group, 16:14; and (5) another Greek group, 16:15. The Gentile believers were now obviously in the majority. Because of Paul's remarks in Romans, written about three years after Jews were permitted back in the city, we conclude that he was fearful that the Gentile Christians were denigrating their Jewish counterparts. In discussing his dismay over the small number of Jews worldwide declaring Jesus as Messiah, and the increasing number of Gentile converts, Paul chided the latter for their tendency to boast (Rom. 11:17-20). He declared that because of their arrogance they themselves might be cut off and believing Jews grafted back in (Rom. 11:21-24). Paul then, was especially concerned that the Gentile believers accept the Jewish minority.

In chapter 14 Paul addressed specific ways in which the outlooks of the weak and the strong were troubling these house churches. The characteristics of the weak imply Jewish predilections. First mentioned is that the weak eat only vegetables (Rom. 14:2). While certain Gentiles may have been vegetarians, the avoidance of meats was the standard approach of punctilious Jews, fearful lest they eat meats dedicated to some deity other than the Lord God. A second item is that the weak judge one day to be better than another (Rom. 14:14). This likely points to Sabbath-keeping as well as the other Jewish feasts. A third practice has to do with what is clean and unclean which seems especially Jewish

(Rom. 14:14). Finally, Paul mentioned abstinence in regard to drinking wine. While most Jews did not abstain, Jews of a Nazirite bent often took a vow to forgo wine, as Paul may have on at least one occasion (Acts 18:18).

Paul tried to allay these frictions by directives and persuasion. Those who seemed overly meticulous were to be welcomed, but not so as to engage in disputes (Rom. 14:1). Paul did not require that the majority rule or that only one practice prevail. Rather, both the weak and strong should continue their commitments, but with toleration on each side. "Those who eat must not despise those who abstain, and those who abstain must not pass judgment on those who eat" (Rom. 14:3). The reason is that God himself has welcomed both (Rom. 14:3). Furthermore, whether the believers eat or abstain, they do it so as to honor the Lord (14:6). Just as Jesus did not live for himself, but died for all, so believers are to live for others and in acceptance of them, as did Christ (Rom. 14:7-9). Persons of different practices and outlooks should be respected and honored because they too are ones "for whom Christ died" (Rom. 14:15). This was especially true since several of the diverse practices counted for little in the sight of God. "For the kingdom of God is not food and drink but righteousness and peace and joy in the Holy Spirit" (Rom. 14:17). In the church therefore, Paul implores, "Let us then pursue what makes for peace and for mutual upbuilding" (Rom. 14:19). One may need to discontinue what she envisions as a harmless activity so as not to cause another to stumble.  ut people who have severe reservations about a practice, whether engaging or sustaining, should never change so as to please a majority. To do so would be a sin (Rom. 14:23).

The strong have the greater responsibility since they are strong. They therefore "ought to put up with the failings of the weak" (Rom. 15:1). That is not to say, however, that Paul privileges the "weak" so that they have every right to demand that their views prevail because of their scruples. The church would constantly be in gridlock if the views of those who object to various proposals are honored. Someone typically objects to every action the church may undertake which is right and good, whether helping the poor, caring for orphans and widows, or assisting in spreading the gospel.

After discussing the specifics Paul concluded, "Welcome one another, therefore, just as Christ has welcomed you, for the glory of God" (Rom. 15:7). Christ welcomed every human into his body regardless of personal traits, ethnic preferences, or diverse life styles. He welcomed them by his death (Rom. 14:9; 15:3). We therefore are summoned to welcome all who are welcomed by Christ. The reason we are to be a welcoming, friendly church is far more profound than simply so that the church may grow. We do it because while we were yet sinners, Christ died for us, as he also died for all who enter our assemblies (Rom. 5:8).

## *The Truth of the Gospel*

Galatians is the letter in which Paul most clearly confronted those who sought to impose Jewish practices upon Gentile converts to Christianity. These intrusions apparently came to a head after Paul left the region. A common assumption is that those pressuring the Galatian Gentile believers to take up a Jewish life style came from Jerusalem, whether or not they were commissioned by the apostles. I am inclined to think that concerns of Jewish parents and relatives living in Galatia could account for the changed attitudes Paul addressed in this letter. From what he wrote, it seems that members within the Galatians churches, no doubt Jewish converts, were trying to persuade Gentile converts to circumcise their sons, and keep the special Jewish festivals. "You are observing special days, and months, and seasons, and years" (Gal. 4:10). These probably included the Sabbath and the Passover. The requirements these troublers were attempting to enforce in most every case Paul designated, "works of the law." Apparently they claimed that the salvation of those who failed to adhere to these regulations might be in jeopardy.

Most of the converts in the Galatian churches were Gentiles (Gal. 4:8-10). But some were Jewish, and these had to bear severe criticism from their Jewish relatives who rejected Paul's teaching. According to Acts, local Jews persecuted Paul in every town in which he planted a church in this region (Acts 13, 14). No doubt the same ill will descended in full force upon the Christians in Galatia. Paul wrote: "It is those who want to make a good showing in the flesh that try to compel you to be circumcised — only that they may not be persecuted for the cross of Christ" (Gal. 6:12). A major scandal among Jewish parents and relatives over those of their own who became members of the Galatian churches was the fact that they ate with the uncircumcised. This practice would have been far more troubling than that they believed in Jesus as the Messiah. Therefore, if the Jewish believers could only persuade the Gentile Christians to be circumcised, they would avoid this major criticism. They could, as a result, inform their relatives that all the Gentile Christians had been circumcised and that they did not, in fact, eat with the uncircumcised! Of course, the Jewish Christians could add even more points should they be able to report that these Gentiles kept the feast days.

Paul contended that the succumbing to these pressures was in fact the denial of the gospel.

> I am astonished that you are so quickly deserting the one who called you in the grace of Christ and are turning to a different gospel — not that there is another gospel, but there are some who are confusing you and want to pervert the gospel of Christ (Gal. 1:6-7).

The truth of the Gospel, according to Paul, resides in faith in Christ. "Yet we know that a person is justified not by the works of the law but through faith in Jesus Christ" (Gal. 2:16).

Paul resisted those who sought to determine whether the ones who came with him to Jerusalem were circumcised, "so that the truth of the gospel might always remain with you" (Gal. 2:5). He also accused Peter and Barnabas, who withdrew from eating with the uncircumcised Christians after an envoy came from Jerusalem, of "not acting consistently with the truth of the gospel" (Gal. 2:14). These important leaders were caving in to the conviction of some that marks on the flesh were important for salvation. Paul argued that salvation is by faith in Jesus as Lord and Savior. To impress upon Gentiles the importance of circumcision is rather to "boast about your flesh" (Gal. 6:13).

Faith in the salvific action of the Son of God is the ground of salvation. Claiming any other ground is a false gospel. Jewish Christians may live like Jews. Paul did not object to that. He essentially remained a practicing Jew all his life. It is likewise appropriate for Gentiles to live like Gentiles. The way of salvation for both Jew and Gentile has nothing to do with life style. It is based upon faith in the death, burial, and resurrection of Jesus Christ. The good news that Christ died for our sins therefore transcends ethnicity. It transcends skin color. It transcends any fleshly differences. The truth of the gospel is that all humans are accepted by God and one in the church because of faith in Christ.

Strong preaching today should denounce the same enemies in kind that Paul denounced at Galatia. My father-in-law, who seldom discussed racial relations, once told me that a black brother, where he went to church, would make an excellent deacon, but he was not appointed because he was black. He proposed the brother's appointment to the leaders, but they took no action. Was their failure to act, on Paul's grounds, not a failure to support the truth of the gospel? Brothers who cave in because of these fleshly distinctions "pervert the gospel of Christ" (Gal. 1:7), or as Paul put it in Galatians 2:5, deny "the truth of the gospel." It is amazing that twentieth-century Christians have accused those who seek to integrate the churches of proclaiming a "social gospel." Paul, in contrast, identified the acceptance of all persons because of faith in Jesus Christ, and regardless of exterior marks, "the true gospel!"

It is of interest that Paul was much more concerned with identifying false brothers on social matters than according to how a brother lines up on the issues, which mostly relate to worship and who is privileged to direct it in the assembly. Have we misfocused Paul's gospel in our worry over apostasy and false brethren? For Paul, the truth of the gospel results in our welcoming people from every race, clime and gender into the church of the Lord Jesus Christ. "There is no longer Jew or Greek, there is no longer slave or free, there is no longer male and female; for all of you are one in Christ Jesus" (Gal. 3:28). Our God, through Jesus Christ, demonstrated that he is no respecter of persons.

## *The Common Meal*

The Christians at Corinth were divided on various fronts. In part, they identified in conclaves with different preachers of note. On these factions Paul commented, "Has Christ been divided? Was Paul crucified for you? Or were you baptized in the name of Paul?" (1 Cor. 1:13). But of more importance, apparently, was that the Corinthians relished flashy gifts of the Spirit. They ranked believers in accordance with the miraculous gift each exhibited. We have already noticed Paul's perspectives on the gifts.

Another manner in which distinctions were apparent was along socioeconomic lines. In regard to their eating the Lord's supper Paul wrote, "When you come together it is not for the better but for the worse. For, to begin with, when you come together as a church, I hear that there are divisions among you . . ." (1 Cor. 11:17-18). The manner in which they were eating, rather than showing unity, placarded differences. "When you come together, it is not really to eat the Lord's supper. For when the time comes to eat, each of you goes ahead with your own supper, and one goes hungry and another becomes drunk" (1 Cor. 11:20-21).

The early Christians either had to meet early in the morning as evidenced from Pliny's letter to the Roman emperor Trajan, or toward evening as the day came to a close. According to Pliny they met at both times. It was not until almost three hundred years later that Constantine the first "Christian emperor" declared Sunday as a day for Christian worship and relatively free from commercial activities. In all likelihood those who came to the assembly early were the more affluent. They brought the best food and wine. Eating commenced soon after these persons higher on the socioeconomic scale arrived. As the shadows crept over the city, servants and slaves trickled into the house where the believers met. They had been involved in house cleaning and food preparing, or in summer harvesting grains, and in fall picking grapes and olives. They had little to bring, and by the time they arrived, most of the food and drink were gone, and they had to go without. "One goes hungry and another becomes drunk" (1 Cor. 11:21), Paul chided them. "What! Do you not have homes to eat and drink in? Or do you show contempt for the church of God and humiliate those who have nothing?" (1 Cor. 11:22).

The assembly proceeded, according to Paul, in the following manner. When they commenced eating they took a loaf of bread, broke it, and shared it. Then they ate a common meal. "In the same way he took the cup also, after supper, saying . . ." (1 Cor. 11:25). So the practice was first the breaking of the bread, then the common or *agape* meal, then after the meal the taking of the cup. The *agape* meal or love feast is also attested to in Jude 12. Because of increasing abuse and no doubt too the growing number of believers, the love feast as a practice declined and some bishops in the second century banned it altogether. Paul's solution to the problem of the fractured assembly was that the believers wait before eating until everyone arrived. If waiting posed a problem because those who came early became hungry, then "eat at home, so that when you come together, it will not be for your condemnation" (1 Cor. 11:33-34). The assembly is the place to show unity in Christ, for he came not only to bring at-one-ment with the Father but with the children of the Father.

All humans are one because they possess the image of God (Jas. 3:9). In Christ, an additional incentive makes it imperative that believers treat each other with respect. Each human is one likewise for whom Christ has died (1 Cor. 8:11). Christ came to reconcile to God those who confess him, and at the same time reconcile one human with another.

# Questions for Discussion

1. How does Acts 2 indicate that Christ reconciled humans to each other?

2. How was Peter convinced that God does not show partiality?

3. What import did Claudius' driving the Jews out of Rome have on the church in Rome?

4. Were there house churches in Rome of a singular ethnic group?

5. Why do the strong have the greater responsibility?

6. Should the conscience of those who object always be honored?

7. Why should we greet people at church?

8. What was the other gospel which some in Galatia attempted to force upon the Gentile converts?

9. How might we be guilty of the same misappropriation?

10. Is preaching on racial prejudice preaching the social gospel?

11. How can the Lord's supper be observed so as to show oneness in Christ?

12. Why did Paul say that the hungry need to first eat at home?

# 13
# He's Coming Back to Claim His Own

When the Son of Man comes in his glory, and all the
angels with him, then he will sit on the throne of his glory.
All the nations will be gathered before him (Matt. 25:31).

The Scriptures of Israel are replete with eschatological (from the Greek *eschatos*, that is "end things")
expectations, and the visions are various. Sometimes writers
foresee horrendous destruction "on that day" because of the
faithlessness of God's chosen (Zeph. 1:10-16). Contrariwise, in
the latter days the God of the heavenly armies (*Yahweh
Sabbaoth*) will vindicate his people (Isa. 25:6-10). Certain
prophets foresaw a new anointed king, unlike any who had
gone before, "And they shall live secure, for now he shall be
great to the ends of the earth; and he shall be the one of peace"
(Micah 5:2-4). In Malachi's vision, evildoers will be consumed
and the righteous healed on the designated day (Mal. 4:1-2).

Jesus resolutely embraced a cataclysmic inbreaking of
God as the driving force of his ministry. "From that time Jesus
began to proclaim, 'Repent, for the kingdom of heaven has
come near'" (Matt. 4:17). We have already seen that Jesus
declared the kingdom of God present in his ministry (Matt.

201

12:28). Furthermore, in the church of Jesus Christ, the kingly power of God through his Holy Spirit has descended upon earth, even though the fountainhead remains in heaven. In the era of the church the kingdom has arrived. The Prince of peace now rules from his heavenly seat of honor. But this one taken up will return at the end of the age, so as to consummate human history. At that time the present evil age will come to a close (Acts 3:19-21).

## *Therefore Keep Watch*

Toward the end of Matthew, Jesus announced to the disciples that the magnificent temple refurbished by Herod the Great would be destroyed. "Not one stone will be left here upon another; all will be thrown down" (Matt. 24:2). Whereupon the disciples asked him both about the destruction of the temple and the end of the age. In regard to the temple Jesus refrained from setting out an exact time, but declared that many false messiahs would arise, wars would be waged as well as rumors of others, and famines and earthquakes would occur. The disciples will be tortured and put to death. Many believers will fall away. False prophets will appear and lead people astray. But in the meantime the good news of the kingdom of God will be proclaimed to all nations (Matt. 24:14). Before the temple is torn down, it will be desecrated as predicted by Daniel. It will be a terrible moment for those involved and those able must flee Jerusalem. The destruction of the temple in Jerusalem by the Romans occurred in A.D. 70, and according to the Jewish historian Josephus it was a time of terror and starvation.

Jesus then addressed the question regarding the end. It will be after the destruction of Jerusalem and terrible portents will precede it, such as darkening of the luminaries and the fall of stars. In the midst of these phenomena the Son of Man will come on the clouds of heaven. He will send out angels to gather his elect from one end of heaven to the other (Matt. 24:30-31).

Human inclination, then and now, is to figure out the exact time of the end. Seismologists consult seismographs around the clock to determine when the next big earthquake will occur. Meteorologists scrutinize weather charts so as to pinpoint the time of hurricanes and tornadoes. Economists pour over fiscal data so as to forecast economic highs and lows. Those who profess expertise in the ways of God likewise prognosticate the precise time of the end. Jesus affirmed that the end will be preceded by signs, but of the specific day and hour no one knows, only the Father (Matt. 24:36). Noah did not know precisely when the rains would commence, but he put out every effort so as to be ready. Life will proceed as normal right up to the end (Matt. 24:39). Everyone will be in for a grand surprise. Those unprepared will be terrified, while the faithful will overflow with joy. Had the home owner known the exact time the thief planned to break in, she would have stationed police at the door (Matt. 24:43).

Since the *eschaton* or end may interrupt life at any moment, according to Jesus, the key to right living is preparedness. "Therefore you also must be ready, for the Son of Man is coming at an unexpected hour" (Matt. 24:44). Just how is one to prepare? The one who is ready will be watchful. How is one to watch? Does it mean that an eye is turned constantly heavenward so as to apprehend the first ray of extraordinary light on the horizon? Does it mean the endless monitoring of news reports so as to ferret out new developments in Israel and the Middle East? No on all counts. Preparedness has to do with being faithful to the tasks God assigned.

> "Who then is the faithful and wise slave, whom his master has put in charge of his household, to give the other slaves their allowance of food at the proper time? Blessed is that slave whom his master will find at work when he arrives. Truly I tell you, he will put that one in charge of all his possessions" (Matt. 24:45-47).

The eyes of the watchful are fixed on their own horizons; neither heavenward nor across the nations. "The righteous live by their faith" (Hab. 2:4). The watchful conscientiously carry out their assigned job description, that is, "caretaker." They are charged with seeing that their associates are fed both bread from earthly grains and the bread of life. The Lord's servants who are derelict in duty through mistreatment of their fellows will be appropriately punished (Matt. 24:48-51).

Parables regarding the ten bridesmaids and the talents in Matthew 25 make the same point. Jesus ended his remarks about end things by describing the separation of the sheep and goats in the grand and final judgment. To those prepared, the King declared,

> "Come, you that are blessed by my Father, inherit the kingdom prepared for you from the foundation of the world; for I was hungry and you gave me food, I was thirsty and you gave me something to drink, I was a stranger and you welcomed me, I was naked and you gave me clothing, I was sick and you took care of me, I was in prison and you visited me" (Matt. 25:34-36).

The righteous, puzzled, asked the Lord when they had done all these things. He replied, "Truly I tell you, just as you did it to one of the least of these who are members of my family, you did it to me" (Matt. 25:40). These people did not have their eyes on the skies or their ears immediately picking up on every newscast regarding the Near East. Their eyes were on their companions. They were immersed in serving just as Jesus served. They were even oblivious to whatever rewards Jesus might dispense in the end time.

The church is to be constantly alert, anticipating the return of its crucified and resurrected Lord. Believers are fed by him from week to week "until he comes" (1 Cor. 11:26). No one who eats at the table of the Lord ever leaves hungry. In turn, the filled ones are to persistently feed others. The faithful are ever cognizant of both the impending end and their assigned employment until it occurs. As Tony Campolo put it:

> Any theology that does not live with a sense of the immediate return
> of Christ is a theology that takes the edge off the urgency of faith. But
> any theology that does not cause us to live as though the world will
> be here for thousands of years is a theology that leads us into social
> irresponsibility.[1]

## To Wait for His Son from Heaven

Paul expected the imminent return of Christ Jesus, though whether it would occur in his own lifetime he did not profess to know. He taught his converts "to wait for his Son from heaven, whom he raised from the dead — Jesus, who rescues us from the wrath that is coming" (1 Thess. 1:10). After Paul left Thessalonica, apparently certain of the believers died. Paul wanted those alive to understand the ramifications. What about the dead? Will they participate with Christ when he returns? Yes, indeed, Paul declared for "Through Jesus, God will bring with him those who have died" (1 Thess. 4:14). The dead will not be left in the grave nor will they be disadvantaged as compared with the living. "For this we declare to you by the word of the Lord, that we who are alive, who are left until the coming of the Lord, will by no means precede those who have died" (1 Thess. 4:15). In this statement Paul may hold open the prospect that he himself will be alive when the Lord returns.

The end will come with a trumpet blast and the descent of the reigning Lord. But of the day or hour no one knows. He will come as a thief in the night (1 Thess. 5:2).

Faithful members of the body will pursue their vocation in him and be prepared for his arrival. "But you, beloved, are not in darkness, for that day to surprise you like a thief . . . . So then let us not fall asleep as others do, but let us keep awake and be sober" (1 Thess. 5:4-6). Paul does not commit himself as to the

---

[1] "Interview: Tony Campolo," *The Door* (September/October 1993): 14.

state of the believers between death and the return of the Lord, but whatever their situation, he declared with expectant hope, that "whether we are awake or asleep we may live with him" (v. 10). Christ's resurrection is the assurance of the believer's involvement in the new age of God, since he "gave himself for our sins to set us free from the present evil age" (Gal. 1:4).

In 2 Thessalonians Paul returned to details regarding the end. Here he emphasized the destruction coming upon those who afflict the believers (2 Thess. 1:6-8).

He also wrote to counter what he had apparently heard, that some, excited by his emphasis on the return, were overly anticipatory. In fact, certain persons went so far as to claim that the day of the Lord had already occurred. As to in what way the return was experienced by those who made the claim is not clear. Paul countered that obvious challenges to the newly founded churches would precede the return. "Let no one deceive you in any way; for that day will not come unless the rebellion comes first and the lawless one is revealed, the one destined for destruction" (2 Thess. 2:3). It is not now obvious who the lawless one is, whether an individual, the Roman empire, or perhaps Satan himself. Apparently Paul had carefully instructed the Thessalonians as to his identity. It may be that some who believed Christ had returned ceased working and were relying on other Christians to supply their needs. Paul bluntly avowed, "Anyone unwilling to work should not eat" (2 Thess. 3:10). A later reference to teachers who claimed that the end had already arrived may be found in 2 Timothy 2:17-18: "Among them are Hymenaeus and Philetus, who have swerved from the truth by claiming that the resurrection has already taken place."

## Christ Is the End of the Law

In Romans, Paul mapped out human history from the beginning to the end. The human plight commenced with

Adam, the first man. Adam sinned, as have all humans since. The first major time span or dispensation was from Adam to Moses (Rom. 5:14). In this era sin was rampant even though torah or law was absent (5:13). The second span was from Moses to Christ, characterized by the Mosaic covenant as a set of guidelines for the people of Israel. Paul entertained the prospect that during the Mosaic era, Gentiles who did not possess the law, might instinctively do what the law requires (Rom. 2:14). Finally Christ came, "born of a woman, born under the law" (Gal. 4:4), bringing in a new era in which salvation for both Jew and Gentile is by grace through faith. The Christian epoch will end when the Lord returns.

Major events must transpire, however, before that momentous culmination of human history. We noticed in 2 Thessalonians that before the end the lawless one will wreak havoc. Paul did not discuss such cataclysmic developments in Romans. He focused instead on a major, yet to occur, embracing of Christ by numerous Jews who as yet had been holding back. Paul believed that his own people were the favored ones. They had all the advantages but they were slow to accept Christ as the Messiah. They had not yet perceived that "Christ is the end of the law." Paul, by "end of the law," apparently meant, first, that Christ was the goal toward which the law aimed, and second, that through his death and resurrection he opened up a new relationship with God unavailable through the law. Paul was impressed with the sizable number of Gentiles who had accepted Christ as Lord, but was notably puzzled about his own people.

Paul reasoned that despite the meager response, God had not actually rejected Israel, for some Jews believed in Christ, himself included (Rom. 11:1). How then is this unusual turn of events to be explained? Paul found clues in the Scriptures. He believed that God hardened the hearts of the majority of the Jews so that a window of opportunity could be opened for the Gentiles (Rom. 11:7-10). After seeing the entry of so many Gentiles into the rapidly expanding kingdom of God, Paul believed that the Jews would become jealous and turn to Christ in droves. He asserted that eventually the full number of Gentiles would enter the kingdom of God, though not every last Gentile, but as many as would receive Christ. Then likewise all of Israel, that is, all of those disposed to receive Christ, would be saved (Rom. 11:25-27). Paul was certain that God was not yet through with his chosen people, Israel. Just how long Paul thought it might take for these ten thousands of conversions is not clear. But he apparently assumed that, as God willed, the turn around could occur almost overnight.

Whatever the details, Paul was persistent in his belief that Christians are under eschatological imperatives. "Besides this, you know what time it is, how it is now the moment for you to wake from sleep. For salvation is nearer to us now than when we became believers; the night is far gone, the day is near" (Rom. 13:11-12). To the Philippians he wrote, "Rejoice in the Lord always; again I will say, Rejoice. Let your gentleness be known to everyone. The Lord is near" (Phil. 4:4-5). In 2 Corinthians Paul no longer considered his survival until the return of the Lord mandatory. On one occasion he felt so crushed that he feared for his very life (2 Cor. 1:8). He seemed more reconciled to the fact that his earthly tent might indeed be destroyed (2 Cor. 5:1).

In Philippians it appears, though not with absolute certainty, that for Paul, the believer does not await the final trumpet call, but upon death immediately goes to be with the Lord.

> For to me, living is Christ and dying is gain. If I am to live in the flesh, that means fruitful labor for me; and I do not know which I prefer. I am hard pressed between the two: my desire is to depart and be with Christ, for this is far better; but to remain in the flesh is more necessary for you (Phil. 1:21-24).

Paul constantly reminded his companions to live in anticipation that the Lord might come at any moment. He did not claim to know the precise time or all the details pertaining to it. He was convinced, however, of the need to be prepared. "So let us not grow weary in doing what is right, for we will reap at harvest time, if we do not give up. So then, whenever we have an opportunity, let us work for the good of all, and especially for those of the family of faith" (Gal. 6:9).

## *The Lord Is Not Slow about His Promises*

As the years wore on, certain believers began to doubt the Lord's return. They had been informed that it would be imminent, but decades went by and nothing happened.

> First of all you must understand this, that in the last days scoffers will come, scoffing and indulging their own lusts and saying, "Where is the promise of his coming? For ever since our ancestors died, all things continue as they were from the beginning of creation!" (2 Pet. 3:3-4).

It could be that among the scoffers were those who held that whatever end there might be had already arrived in some nonempirical fashion. Regardless, Peter guaranteed his readers that however slow, they should rest assured that God, in his own good time will end history, and every last person will know it.

In the long ago past God, by his word, created the heavens and formed earth out of water. Later by that same water, due to sin and the ensuing deluge, the earth perished. No one who was alive at that time failed to observe the flood (2 Pet. 3:6). Sometime in the future the heavens and the earth will be consumed by fire (2 Pet. 3:7). That grand conflagration will be seen by all alike. How long will it be until this final holocaust arrives? Peter did not pinpoint a date. But it may be a long time, and if so, it will be in order that many more will come to repentance (2 Pet. 3:8-9).

The day on which the heavens and the earth will be destroyed, and will slip up unawares like a thief in the night, "then the heavens will pass away with a loud noise, and the elements will be dissolved with fire, and the earth and everything that is done on it will be [burned up]" (2 Pet. 3:10). Beyond that mass burn off God will create anew. "But, in accordance with his promise, we wait for new heavens and a new earth, where righteousness is at home" (2 Pet. 3:13). The vision of a new heaven and a new earth was announced by Isaiah. "For I am about to create new heavens and a new earth" (Isa. 65:17).

Peter, as did all the New Testament writers, believed that the prospect of a fiery consummation injected a strong sense of urgency into human existence.

> Therefore, beloved, while you are waiting for these things, strive to be found by him at peace, without spot or blemish; and regard the patience of our Lord as salvation (2 Pet. 3:14).

When the church espouses the conclusion that its Lord may be long delayed, it drifts endlessly on a sea of inaction and complacency. It is like those who file one income tax extension after another. They feel little pressured by the urgency of the deadlines. Procrastinators constantly put off the moment of action, and will ultimately face the ire of God.

## The Lion of the Tribe of Judah Has Conquered

The book of Revelation has been mined more than any other in the New Testament for the purpose of ascertaining what lies over the horizon. According to some commentators almost every prediction in the book came to fruition by A.D. 70. In fact, the introductory remarks profess that the revelation is of what must soon take place (Rev. 1:1). "The revelation of Jesus Christ, which God gave him to show his servants what must soon take place . . . ." But many interpreters through history have assumed that many projections in the book have long-range implications. The author assumes that most aspects of human events are hidden. God therefore has given Jesus Christ, and through him to John, the means thereby to decipher what is unknown. These insights are disclosed through angels with trumpets, candlesticks, seals, scrolls, and many other symbols. These many phenomena themselves indicate the cryptic nature of the information. Those who profess to unravel these deep mysteries attack these symbols with great aplomb, but seldom with unanimity.

Whatever the details mean, the basic story line of Revelation is clear. The future of history has already been planned out. God has set the wheels in motion so that despite ominous opposition, Christ will win the final cosmic battles hands down. In an early cryptic scene, the Lord God, seated on a dazzling throne, held a scroll in his right hand with writing on the inside, and seven seals on the back. An angel in a loud voice asked, "Who is worthy to open the scroll and break its seals?" (Rev. 5:2). But no one on earth or under the earth was able. John began to weep bitterly because he concluded that the secrets contained therein would never be known. Then one of the elders consoled John, "Do not weep. See, the Lion of the tribe of Judah, the Root of David, has conquered, so that he can open the scroll and its seven seals" (Rev. 5:5). Because of the victory of Christ, the key to the future is available, as well as God's ability to bring history to his desired conclusion.

A teacher of the unchurched met regularly with a young woman for Bible study. After some months, she decided to put on Christ in baptism and the arrangements were made. She informed her teacher the night before, that she planned to read through Revelation. He was somewhat taken aback and his first impulse was to discourage her, thinking that she would likely end up confused. But instead, he responded, "Sounds good." The next day, with some trepidation, he asked, "Well, what did you learn?" She responded in great confidence, "I learned that our side wins." Her conclusion, despite the cryptic symbols in Revelation, as well as the somewhat ambiguous disclosures, is perhaps the singular consensus among all who comment on the work.

In the twentieth century many interpreters of Revelation argue for a composition date during the reign of Domitian (A.D. 81-96) or about A.D. 95. But others who argue that the destruction of Jerusalem in A.D. 70 is yet future when Revelation was written, prefer the reign of Nero (A.D. 54-68). The common presumption, in view of the mention of martyrs, is that persecution to Christians has already occurred. The oppressors most likely are officials of some Roman political entity (Rev. 6:9-10; compare Rev. 11:7-13).

Later in Revelation the perpetrator of these atrocities takes the form of a beast with two horns thought to symbolize Nero (Rev. 13:11). Next the imagery of the oppressor is changed to that of a great whore sitting on a beast with seven heads and ten horns. The seven heads are taken to represent the seven hills of Rome and the 10 horns ten emperors. Finally the great city Babylon, obviously a cryptic name for Rome, will be destroyed (Rev. 18:1-3).

The final defeat of Rome occurred when a rider, who is obviously Jesus Christ, appeared on a white horse (Rev. 19:11, cf. 6:2). At his arrival the beast and the kings of the earth gathered with their armies to make war. But they were no match for the rider on the white horse. The beast was captured along with the false prophet. These two were thrown into the lake of fire and their supporting armies killed with the sword (Rev 19:20). The defeat of these evil forces represented the first stage of the end. The most magnificent empire ever created by humans was now destroyed. Christ was hands down the victor.

The next stage of the battle had cosmic ramifications. An angel came down from heaven, seized Satan, bound him and threw him into the pit for a thousand years (Rev. 20:2). After his millennial incarceration he was released for a time. At this point commentators offer many interpretations. Some, as I have said, argue that these thousand year spans are not to be taken literally. These millennia represent periods in the first century. But persons of a premillennial outlook adamantly believe in an actual thousand-year binding of Satan, a continuation of the nations, and a thousand-year reign of Christ with the faithful on earth. When the thousand years are ended, Satan will be released and go forth to deceive the nations (Rev. 20:7-9). All the mighty armies on the earth will encamp about the saints and their beloved city, but suddenly their threats will end when fire falls from heaven and devours them. At that point Satan will be thrown into the lake of fire along with the beast and the false prophet (Rev. 20:10).

Now that the cosmic powers of evil are defused and sealed off, God is revealed on a great white throne. So awesome is he that everything flees from his presence. The dead are brought before his throne and judged. Those declared evil are cast, along with Death and Hades, into the lake of fire (20:14). The first heaven and the first earth at that time also passed away (Rev. 21:1).

Once all the evil was cordoned off, John saw a new heaven and a new earth and the new Jerusalem coming down out of heaven from God (Rev. 21:1-2). God's holy city is to occupy the new earth and God himself will reign in the midst of his people. Reconciliation is now complete. Humankind will dwell with God in complete empathy.

> He will dwell with them as their God;
> they will be his peoples,
> and God himself will be with them;
> he will wipe every tear from their eyes.
> Death will be no more;
> mourning and crying and pain will be no more,
> for the first things have passed away (Rev. 21:3-4).

In this new city God will be all in all. No temple is needed. No sun or moon is required. God supplies both worship and light (Rev. 21:22-24). In this city the tree of life may be seen in all its eminence. No longer will mortals be barred from its fruit (Rev. 22:2). They shall eat and live forever.

What then has become of evil? "Nothing accursed will be found there any more. But the throne of God and of the Lamb will be in it, and his servants will worship him; they will see his face, and his name will be on their foreheads" (Rev. 22:3-4). Does this mean that nothing accursed will be in the city, or that since everything accursed has been thrown into the lake of fire, that all manner of evil has been consumed once for all and no longer exists? The latter is a possible interpretation. God has never punished for the sake of punishing alone. He is no medieval craftsman who relishes the construction of torture devices. God does not delight in punishment. Rather, he has dedicated himself to creating a kingdom of love, goodness and beauty. In order to achieve this end, he has been at work from time immemorial ridding all realities of hatred, cruelty and ugliness, now and forevermore.

## Conclusion

The story line of the New Testament announces that the God who struggled endlessly with Israel broke into history in a new way in the Son, Jesus Christ. In him the age-old alienation of humans with each other and with the Divine are overcome. He came as Savior, not only of Israel, but of all who receive him. Because of God's gracious gift in the Son, humanity ever since should be focused upon and serious about emulating him.

> For Christ's love compels us, because we are convinced that one died for all, and therefore all died. And he died for all, that those who live should no longer live for themselves but for him who died for them and was raised again (2 Cor. 5:14-15, NIV).

# Questions for Discussion

1. What are the backgrounds for Jesus' declaration that the kingdom of God has come near?

2. How did Jesus depict the time and details of the destruction of the temple?

3. What did Jesus teach as the appropriate way to watch for his return?

4. On what basis will believers be judged in the end time?

5. What happens to a church that thinks the return of Christ may be hundreds of years away?

6. What does Paul offer for insight as to the circumstances of those believers who have died?

7. On what basis did certain early Christians declare that the day of the Lord had already arrived?

8. How did Paul map out the long course of history and its end?

9. Did Paul think that God was through with his people Israel?

10. What do you conclude as to the imminent return of Christ in 2 Peter?

11. What is the basic story line of Revelation?

12. What events must occur before the New Jerusalem is let down from heaven according to Revelation?

# About the Author

Thomas H. Olbricht was born in Thayer, Missouri. He received degrees from Northern Illinois University, the University of Iowa, and Harvard Divinity School. He has served Churches of Christ as a minister in Illinois, Iowa, Massachusetts, and Pennsylvania and as an elder in Abilene, Texas, and Malibu, California. Olbricht has taught at Harding University, The University of Dubuque, The Pennsylvania State University, Abilene Christian University, and Pepperdine University from which he retired in 1996. He has published ten books, written articles in fifty others, and has served as editor of and published in several journals. He and Dorothy, his wife of almost fifty years, live in South Berwick, Maine. They have five children and twelve grandchildren.

College Press Publishing Company, Inc.

Other Books By Thomas Olbricht:
*He Loves Forever*

Related Titles Published by College Press:
*Falling in Love with Jesus* by Rubel Shelly
*Yet Will I Trust Him* by John Mark Hicks

*College Press produces Bible Commentaries,
Small Group Studies, Sunday School Materials,
Vacation Bible School Materials, and Christian
Books on a variety of topics.
To See These Products:*

**Contact Your Local Bookstore**

Or

College Press Publishing Company, Inc.
**1-800-289-3300** Toll Free
email ***books@collegepress.com***
Visit our web page at
**www.collegepress.com**